Praise for
AMERICAN ENTROPY

"Hupp's must-read transformative poems, filled with depth and raw emotion, reach into the core of your being. You will find yourself re-visiting them to peel away layers that may have been missed during the first reading. I found reading them aloud with a partner prompted profound discussion as well."

– Rebecca Colt Aslan, author of *Some Truths Lie Beneath*

"From a marginalized group Hupp takes aim at the political issues of today, using poetics to vent his understandable rage at the hypocrisy now at the surface of society, a hypocrisy which has always existed, since society is composed of humans. Full of imaginative, poetic imagery and metaphors, this ebullient and brutally honest collection of poetry follows Thomas Paine, who said, 'The pen is mightier than the sword.'"

– Linda Marie Hilton, author of *Words of a Feather Hawked Together*

AMERICAN ENTROPY

AMERICAN ENTROPY
POEMS

TRAVIS HUPP

atmosphere press

© 2025 Travis Hupp

Published by Atmosphere Press

Cover design by Kevin Stone
Cover art by Michael Sizemore

No part of this book may be reproduced without permission from the author except in brief quotations and in reviews.

Atmospherepress.com

AUTHOR'S NOTE

My bad dreams are expansive in thematic material these days. I dream we're all on trump's enemies list and he's jailing or executing anyone who won't undermine the Constitution for him, but that's just one of a gamut of varied terrors that lurk in sleep. I also dream that Christian fundamentalist "good old boys" are stoning me to death to show me how they feel about an openly gay man like myself returning to Christianity after 20-plus years spent as an apostate. There are dreams where something unseen is just behind me, breathing on my neck, climbing onto my back, letting loose an unhinged cackle as it exerts impossible pressure on my body, holding me helpless as the walls around me sprout necrotic gray arms, reaching out to pull me into some nether realm. That last example is likely influenced by the things I hear when I'm fully awake and lucid; the voices I hear that others don't, which rasp that I better not go outside at night, that they're always watching. That they're going to kill my dogs. That they're trying to drive me to suicide. Those are just a few of their common refrains. I've been dealing with these intrusive auditory manifestations (be they hallucinations or communication from a stronghold of low, frenzied demons) for years now. It's increasingly hard to remember a time when it was just me in my head.

Despite all this, I'm full of optimism for the future. Because for a while now, other voices have been coming through, too. There are voices that tell me that not everything in the other realms is twisted and murderous. Voices that cheer me on when I stand up for myself, and laugh with me at the banal, dimwitted depravity of my demonic antagonists, who are growing increasingly frustrated about their shtick being too rote by now to be scary. These friendly voices make good allies in the war to reclaim my mind. Lately they've been singing softly to me when I pray, and the closer their voices sound, the more I feel what I can only describe as a jubilant warm glow bloom in the center of my body.

There's no proof that God sent angels to rescue me from infiltrating demons, but that's what happened. I can't prove that I'm not just tripping balls all the time, but what I can tell you is that multiple psychiatrists and psychologists have told me they don't think I'm schizophrenic or suffering from DID. Drug use may very well have played a part in developing this condition, but is that because drugs open your third eye or because drugs alter your brain chemistry? Does changed brain chemistry *really* explain what's happening to me any better than just calling it psychic or spiritual phenomena does? I believe I hear Heaven singing when I pray. I turned to God in peril of insanity, when the demonic voices threatened to overwhelm me, and He hasn't been subtle about saving me. I wonder, if the demons had known they were just going to end up bolstering my faith and restoring my sense of wonder, would they still have targeted me? Now they seem like they're stuck here with me and unsure what to do.

So maybe it's understandable that the demons are getting crowded out of my nightmares, replaced by visions of things like trump's hungry, empty totalitarianism running rampant. There are poems in this collection I wrote back when the demons were still intimidating, but when I turn my poetry on trump, you might find the malevolence more oppressive. What he's done to the structural integrity of everything that holds American society together is so horrible that I can't even bring myself to show him the basic respect of capitalizing his name. Not to dehumanize him, especially after he was nearly assassinated twice; I just don't respect racism, sexism, transphobia, homophobia, or trying to steal elections.

Optimism aside, I can't deny we're living in scary times. The country is divided against itself along more lines than ever. Loneliness is an epidemic we seek to alleviate with technology that seems to drive us further apart . Many of us either don't believe in God or we believe that God is a homophobe. Believers and atheists call each other arrogant and dim, because it's easier than listening to each other. Science is frowned on by fundamentalists that can't see God at work in it. Religious belief is treated like borderline insanity by those who think scientific belief demands strict atheism. The percentage of Americans who think political violence is justifiable keeps climbing. Guns outnumber people. The signs of American entropy are all around us, all the time.

Still, I believe we can snatch democracy back from the brink, reinforce the pillars of society weakened by a lying charlatan acting in bad faith, rediscover unity of spirit and stop deceiving ourselves into thinking that science and God are antithetical to one another. I still think it's a smart bet to believe in God and each other. I even still believe in falling in love in a society that tries to drill it into my head that me doing so is a sin that will be punished.

Every day, I face down demons, I commune with angels, I coax out the poetry of American entropy, finding in it those things that refuse to fall away.

Whoever you are — whatever your sexual orientation, race, gender identity or faith — thank you for reading my poetry and taking this journey with me. May the angels always sing to you when you most need them.

TABLE OF CONTENTS

ANGER

THE FIGHT IN THE GUY	3
A WOUND AWARE	5
ENEMY EMBRACE	6
UNCLENCH	8
INNOCENT ENOUGH	10
ECHO IN THE AFTERGLOW	11
WHOEVER YOU ARE	13
THE DIRECT RESULT	14

POLITICS

TALKING SENSE	17
GORGED	20
THE REAL WAVEMAKERS	22
SCREAMING PENITENTS	27
ENDLESS TRAUMA	28
IT'S COME TO EXILE	29
BREAKING DOWN	31
TOLERANCE	32
THE STOCKADE	34
MARTYR	36
INNER BALDWIN	40
THE WORST ONE	42

METAPHYSICAL

87% OF THE TIME IN THE SIMULATION	47
SIGNALINGS	49
EDGEWISE	51

FINAL SHRINE	53
ONLY THE UNDERTOW	54
I'M LOST IF YOU'RE LOST	56
SHRUG	59
AND	61
GONE	62
I STRIVE	64
INTERSECTIONS	65
DID THIS TO YOURSELF	67
THE SPIRIT MOVES	68
VEILS	70
SECRET KNOWLEDGE	72
THE BACK FOOT	73
ZOMBIED	75
DELIVER ME	76
LIFEBREATH	77
THE ETHER	79
A FEATURE AND A BUG	80
ROUGH WEATHER PRAYER	90

DESPAIR

LET IT GO	93
CARRYING THE STONE	94
AMERICAN ENTROPY	96
SUNKEN	97
WORDLESSLY	99
CRY DARKLING	101
WITHOUT	103
HORROR SHOW	104
MENTICIDE	106
UPWARD MOBILITY	109
YESTERDAY REPEATING	110
JUST	111
MOVING IN	112

NOTHING LEFT	114
FORGETTING	115
MISCHIEF	116
SCREENS	118
DONE TO DEATH	119
FRANKLY	120
SICK	121
VOCABULARIES	122

HOPE

I'LL HELP YOU FIND IT	125
ON PURPOSE	127
DON'T MAKE ME GET MEAN	128
IT'S NOT TOO LATE	130
METTLE	132
I FEEL A CHANGE	134
THE TRUTH	136
UNTAMED	137
HIVE MIND	140
CELEBRATE YOU	141
ALIVE	144
ULTRA UNDERGROUND	145
RESURRECT	146
MAYBE THIS TIME	148
FINEST KIND	150
THROTTLE	152
HOPE ANYWAY	153
AS I PLEASE	155
IMPOSSIBLE MUSIC	156
PRIMAL POWERS	158
BRING THE HEAT	160
ESCAPE ROUTE	161
BATTLE	163
SOMEPLACE	164

LOVE

WHAT ALL I LIKE	169
VITAL VIBE	171
SIMPATICO	173
A GLIMPSE	175
FAVORITE VILLAIN	176
CONSTANT DAYDREAM	178
HALFWAY	180
BEYOND OUR MEANS	181
DIVE DEEP	183
HAPPIEST	185
THE ULTIMATE EPIC	187
WELL OF WANTING	189
HIS COURAGE	190
NEWS OF FIRES	191
HEARD YOU TELL IT	193
PERCENTAGES	195
SWEAR	197
THE SUM OF US	198
CERTAIN SKULLDUGGERY	200
WONDERSTRUCK	202
STARRY EYES	204
CRACKED OPEN	205
SUMMONERS	207
ROAMING IN YOUR WILDS	209
HAVE TO BUT IT'S HARD	211
CONCEPT OF LOVE	212
SOLID HANG	214
ANYWHERE BUT SPLITSVILLE	215
INEXHAUSTIBLE	216
ABSTRACTION	218

THE FIGHT IN THE GUY

I'll show you how to hustle
from clusterfuck to kerfuffle

Random Schmoes
rabble-rabble-ing at our backs

This is how you do it
Quicken pace
Set mantra to "Screw it"

Unhinged laughs at anyone taken aback

To our discredit
we grow to like getting in fights
What's that they say, though?
"It's the fight in the guy"?

This guy is fighting
to put down his countrymen's petty hate
and this one is fighting
because he's learning to rage

It's the storm you turn on and off
until one day the button gets stuck

You're the volcano
I live on the rim of
The days you erupt are
the days I'm in luck

Running rampant risking ruin
No quarter asked or nothin' doin'

Snap back like an inflatable Skeletor sandbag
and get beaten flat blow by blow
amidst the thrill of throwing hands

Mark it down to
the bill coming due
for malignant murderousness
and complicit ambivalence

This guy is fighting because
he hears what you really think
and this one is fighting
because the two are a team

A WOUND AWARE

Too honest for a general audience
Set you free, what about me
Hypervigilant victim, bravery screams
into the glare and the glinting
of sudden shards falling
A wound aware, fury unflinching
Resonant in your lair
Sudden sharp singing

ENEMY EMBRACE

Nearly knocked cold when the first stone
connected with my forehead
Heard their celebratory chorus
cut the very sky

Maybe there's no crime for which
I've been tried or convicted
but he's winding up to throw another
For lucky aim he kissed it

Can't miss me
Cascading crimson
Judge me, bash my brains
out my nostrils
down the front of my shirt
Still alive
Really asking for it

Can't miss me
Bone showing
Let me have it, cave my skull
into my sinful soul
Make sure it hurts
I don't cry
Won't let you
feel that important

Smile somewhat shattered
Surprisingly sturdy sick ass queer
Standing in the rocky rain
bleeding from both ears

Why stubbornly survive
Murder's not meant
to last all evening
Gash, collapse
I decide to not die easy

No, me, I need my back broke
before bowing or giving ground
the earth he means
to bury me in
I curse to pull him down
After me
Ever locked with me
in an enemy embrace
I won't be firmly planted
'til I get to spit
some blood in his face

UNCLENCH

Looking at me like I must not
be from your galaxy
Screwing your face all up like it
makes you mad at me
I can tell you where I'm from
to the best of my knowledge
We all believe what our parents tell us
or it's existential carnage
But why the reflexive showing of
such a rude tone of face
A pinched scowl so aggressive it
invites reciprocal rage
Like it's your lot alone to put
misanthropes like me in our place
which we should've been born knowing
since it's where we're bred to stay
Someplace cordoned off from
your virtue's vicinity
Where our inhalations can't
poach your air
An abattoir adjacent to absence
A knoll a parsec past nowhere
Well maybe I showed up here
fated to shake your beliefs
Maybe my unkempt non-observance
of your snotty rules
should generate grief
over the loss of societal propriety
The loss of any ghost of good sense
Maybe my destiny's totality is

that I exist to help you unclench
Because I have my own ideas about
where people like each of us belong
Those impoverished but honest and
those well-coiffed who can't get along
I think I'm within my rights to wander
more or less unfettered wherever I like
and you belong in a hidey hole
where the offended convince themselves
fright makes right

INNOCENT ENOUGH

To forgive is divine
First I'll malign this time
Sometimes I can't help it
I'm only a person
Only one of the innocents you're hurting

Not innocent entirely but innocent enough
In this particular context, we're basically doves
But take care, we might molt
into warbirds, merciless and dangerous
Soon you might curse your cruelty for changing us

ECHO IN THE AFTERGLOW

I can hear you listening

I can empathize with your enmity

I can slow dance with
your echo in the afterglow
of the fights we have every evening

I can hurt for both of us

I can second guess every gesture

I can be the comedian
taking whatever pratfalls
might impress you

You can see me watching

You can polish your crystal portents

You can find me in the rubble
and lead me unsuspecting
to the rubbish

You can live for both of us

You can live for us all

You can gluttonize
whole galaxies
Leech their suns cold and dark

I can let you do this

You can't let me not

Bend nearer
Believe me beguiled as
my dagger finds home in your heart

WHOEVER YOU ARE

Why would I even remember you at all
Tell me one good reason, whoever you are
Prod out one good memory, if you even can
from the seedy underbelly of bad juju's
natural habitat

Who would you even say came by to call
Tell me what this season finds your nom de guerre
Rattle the names off that caged you before
The call signs, the rapper handles, the winner
or it's war

Where will you seduce springtime, and where will
your autumn groupies caravan to fall
Quell my hypnic jitters, spill the tea, suss the sauce
Put your power move in the planner
Keep your fandom fibrillating and paying to wait
to see you flip your hair, to snare sips of
your rarified air
Limping to line up, first row from your fresh face
Overplaying strange charades

THE DIRECT RESULT

From this moment on
be grateful I've already killed you
That I've scoured from my soul
every infectious strain of you
That your death in the physical realm
could never compare to
your death in my mind
and know that every breath you breathe
is the direct result of me
refusing to waste my time

TALKING SENSE

Chow down on lies, torture the truth
Never fact check your precious Fox News
You're undermining and maligning intellect
but you know what
Fuck it, steer into the wreck

Death to brains
Death to brains
Death to brains
No need to strain
Death to brains
Death to brains
Let donald explain

When your eyes are a light gone out
I get crestfallen
I'm talking sense, you're preaching poison
You throw such loads it's a wonder
your mouth can hoist them
I'm talking sense but it feels pointless

A hat, MAGA red
A tranquilizer for horses
A Kool-Aid cure
Another sycophant sorted

Into the queue, yeah, into the unskeptical mob
Into the pile of people who would jump on a bomb
to protect every strand of donald's tumbleweed hair

Exploding eagerly, sycophant everywhere

You're really the worst now but I guess
that's how you like it
You're a nationalist now, a hero for whiteness
Our association makes me queasy
I cut you off but it doesn't stick 'cos you're crazy

Death to brains
Death to brains
Death to brains
and to memory
Death to brains
Death to brains
Reality's the enemy

When your face goes slack from
your regularly scheduled brainwash
I know you'll turn it back on
but I gotta try, so I turn it off
I'm talking sense, you're reaching for the remote
Your channel is sacred, it tells you
all you need to know
If I question any of it, you corner me
with non-sequiturs bemoaning American decline
Prophesizing only your orange idol
can turn back that black tide
I'm talking sense but your whole mind's wiped

A Bible he stamped his fleshy face on
An autograph on it, too, 'cos he's your avatar of God
A torrent of a tirade, demonstrably false
A pledge of revenge that doesn't give you pause

I forgot a sycophant could get this sick
You'd burn everything down just to own the libs
It's hard to accept you're so far gone
Serene in the cesspool, indoctrinating your spawn

> Death to brains
> Death to brains
> Death to brains
> You sing along
> Death to brains
> Death to brains
> It's a brand new, dumb dawn

GORGED

Why aren't you working
I don't call that working
To death dear to death
Anything less is apostasy

What's wrong with your retinue
Have you even a retinue
Who let you think poetry
is even anything anyway

It doesn't pay
You must pay
If you make babies
the government will
pay you for each of them
Reproduce because it's
good for the corporations
always needing to replenish
the youth demographic gorged on

A nine to five job
A second six to eight job
That's an hour on each side
to live the rest of your life in

It's for the best
Markets always know what's best
Keep them free and unregulated
Let oligarchs get you relegated

You have to hammer harder
You gotta sell harder
Haven't you heard of
the old hard sell
It's poverty wage here
or poverty wage elsewhere

You don't have the money
to make real money
You're a plaything for
those who can pay
those who get everybody's
cloud paying them

Those the AI work for
who can afford to ask what work's for
Who get to decide what work
for the rest of us
even looks like anyway
They've assured us
anything worthwhile
automatically triggers a windfall

Is it a form of madness
Is it perhaps the most bankrupt madness
Bankrupt like beloved trumpism
Stare into the vacuous void of it
Let it break any tenuous grip
you might have had on
any resonant aftershock
of the art you made
before hard truth remade you
Hell for most of us is worth it
if it means Heaven for a chosen few

THE REAL WAVEMAKERS

It sounds like it looks
know what I mean
It smells like something iffy you step in

Did you know we get the meaning of
"Blood thicker than water" backwards
Did you know we do that shit with a lot of things

Lucky enough to be a voice slinging earfuls, but it seems like
it takes time for word of how I tear it down to get around

Meanwhile Ducky goes down on
enough of the council to establish a quorum
Not to tell anyone else's tale for them
Gotta get in where you fit in
unless everyone just crams in everywhere
or maybe not exactly everywhere
but at least anywhere anyone even tries to be fair

They told Ducky "Know your place"
Ducky didn't though
Ducky puts on a show wherever Ducky goes

Check for what now in whose blood
The doc already knew me to be negative
but didn't tell me 'til I
offered some blood to stay on the safe side

On my first appointment they asked if I'm "a" gay
I said "Fuckin' A!" in gay octaves

so I guess they just tested me automatically
without asking consent or informing me
Guess doctor/patient confidentiality
Isn't exclusive enough as is
so they don't necessarily loop in the patient anymore
How's that shit for a policy shift

If they ask for the same test the doc knows
they no longer need to run
revealing their result is optional then
but with how loose rumor is some subgroups are
They might keep the word mum and just double up

Don't know why I'm so hung up on this
Just thought my health concerned me I guess
No cause for much consternation kid
As long as someone knows how sick I am
or rather (Hallelujah!) how sick I'm not

Hallelujah O'Malley would be a good band name
If naming bands was a job
damn I'd dominate
but don't you know it just takes so long
for word of the real wavemakers to get around

Fact is if anything I want or care about or stand for
or can get behind standing shoulder to shoulder with
turned out to be a real job
I'd careen far in said career
but poetry's what I'm hired for
ever since I named myself hiring manager
I also gave myself the titles of

Overboss and Community Relations Manager
I really make a dynamite team

Oh fine if that's still not a job then
Some would say it counts as a "path" at most
since everyone knows arts don't bankroll
much but a "Who gets the last cracker" lifestyle
It just takes so long to even get one teensy big break

Who does get it though
If I truly believe
can the cracker be for me

Never now it's been so long since
they say I've worked hard
Hard to call it hard work unless it's a shit slog
or fire of at least four and a half alarms

For example you could help head off emergencies untold
by making it your job to test people for all kinds of stuff
so stealthy-like they don't even know

Wonder what else medical professionals have taken initiative on
Any pacemaker or anti-dismayer installed
THINK THINK how micro are micro-incisions
THINK THINK am I missing any time

"Where does it end" was a softball question
When those encounter me they kinda complicate
Whatever an end is and wherever such a
showdown or sewing circle exists
I'll know at least the last cracker was rightfully mine

So then I'll trade it for a nickel right
'cos you're supposed to always make and spend money
preferably at the same time
Everyone knows that
Even "a" gay
Word got around you could even say

Fast forward and I prove capitalism can trust me
Sure enough I traded that morsel for money
My stomach grumbled but I told it
"Sorry, can't eat patriotism!"

Actually, can I get a fact check
here at the alleged end of it all
Is patriotism's consistency gummy or gristle
Does it taste like mouthing off to commie scum
Do true patriots suck patriotism like malt balls

If you work hard enough you get a cracker
or you get to know that once someone got a cracker
You can only hope they did the right thing
The exchange rate is five cents USD

To earn such riches they say
be better than I was told I wasn't yesterday
Then they ask if there's any way I could
be *that* kind of "a" gay
A flamboyant cartoon who theatrically entertains
So I limp up my wrists and they thank me
by informing me I've been tested
for the latest thing in plagues

"Surprise surprise my flaming friend
it's gay panic GAY PANIC GAY PANIC AGAIN!!!!"

Which lucky contestant guessed "gay panic"
For bonus points who can define "twinkie defense"
It appears the winning contestant is everyone
So how come no one
seems to know no one now
Who's been spreading the gossip all over town

Maybe word just gets around
Cos Word is
y'know
"Down to clown"

Betcha Ducky's heard the whole thing by now

SCREAMING PENITENTS

The crash clamps down, the fire drowns
No one knows what anyone's saying anymore
The saga's every subplot eaten up by the roar

For a time innocent, born screaming penitents
Requisite shame attaches before names
To the lash and the firing squad, all meat's the same

The dreamscape attained, all territories claimed
Disputed by watchmen unhindered by vision
Whole histories hidden by glaring omission

For temerity locked up, for your portion none
Milking man's collective malice for anything other
Boots grinding under misfit sister and brother

The locket unadorned, the artist unmourned
Piece by piece, sketching scarcity
Last verses bleed through broken, bared teeth

For a song swindled, feuds bundled and kindled
Revenge exacted by bullet or by blind eye
The terminal tell the tale, no one else survives

ENDLESS TRAUMA

Balmy June
Crude junkies
Nearly ruined
Mother fucking
Earth abused
Extensive damage
Future doomed
Resources mismanaged
Cruelest climate
Affected fauna
Animals endangered
Endless trauma
Human hands
Hardly helping
Little late
Glaciers melting
Oceans brackish
Filmy surface
Deadly oversights
Spilling curses
What survives
Greatly diminished
Fully violated
Finally finished
Oxygen thin
Ozone assassinated
Ecosystem buckling
Gaia exsanguinated

IT'S COME TO EXILE

All month long the muse denudes
your attitude's entitled altitude
Full frontal fuckwit
Hook me up with a full frontal lobotomy
You're whining on an infinite loop
You're standing right on top of me
We're all getting down and riled up
Just letting our inner creatures cavort
Just having some free fun
Nothing sinister
but you're not even trying
to be a good sport
The rest of us are gonna
give roughing it off-grid a chance
Staking our claim
to this forgotten stretch of land
Animals, all of us
Animal agendas we'll advance
It's what's best for
the world picked bare
but you just took
You wouldn't share
If you saw a hand out
you bit the fucker off
So don't start up now
with your hard luck stuff
All about how bad you hurt
How much you lack
How you lost your new job
'cos of panic attacks

Let that learn you your lesson
the tent city mayor commands
Last week you were too upstanding
to try some knock-off candy
You said nothing for you
unless it's name brand
Now you're sweating
a whole 'nother sugar
You're craving a whole 'nother
form of sweet
but no one's got any
kind of sweet for you
'cos both your mouth
and your swagger got mean
So hunch off now
Hound us no further
You're evicted from
this hub of commerce
Evicted from the extra sleeping bag
even if you blubber so much your words slur
You cooked your own roast
and you'll get none of ours
Gussy up your own ghost
'cos you're dead to our hearts
You can't spit shine your face enough
to show a new side
Any chance we take on you
would get us taken for a ride
Sorry it's come to exile
Sorry your new leaves
keep rotting unturned
but you can't toast your digits
around our trashcan anymore
Get outta here before you get burned

BREAKING DOWN

Standardizing the sub-standard
Par for the course is
of course sub-par
Whether they break you down
into colors or graphs or numbers
what you remember is the breaking down
Not what someone else learned from it
Not the affiliation it sequesters you into
Not the always evolving acronym
of your extra special interest
let alone the official title of
the most compatible therapist

TOLERANCE

They say since we created parades
to try and stay safe
our visibility necessitates
a pity party where Pride is straight
Sounds a lot like the event
all of us have always
by default been attending
but when's this shindig starting
I'm excited for the implied ending

They want tax write-offs
for each one of their
oodles of tots
They wanna skim the coin
I won't be slave to the influence of
They wanna hyperjump
their spawning of planet killers
even though Earth's had enough of us

Damn right they're here
to reclaim the rainbow
No sigil can be left in
the corrupt custody of faggots
Lesbians, on the other hand
there's an eagerness to parley with
Not the bulldykes, though
Better send in the lipsticks

The team hasn't played
Smear The Queer in a hot sec
How's that for a triumph of tolerance
What a moral example
about willpower they've
provided to all of us

At least when it comes to commerce
they keep it professional
As long as their customers with dicks
match corresponding clits
Otherwise we're not allowed to shop
in the stores where we live
We just gotta get vouched for
that we've recently been in vagina
or be respectfully denied service
by any reasonable Christian proprietor

What more can we expect
Always forcing things down throats
with our lurid hugging in public
How can we exist
in oodles of our own
when no Republicans even
signed our permission slips

THE STOCKADE

Baby believer, destroy this infidel
They insist on the right pronouns
They act according to their nature

Baby believer, kill this socialist
They won't trust capitalism
to make the most of their talents and passions

Make them change their tune
or shun them to the stockade
Make them sing my verses
Make them play my game

Baby believer, nurse that crush on my celebrity
Feed it 'til it bloats
Quicker, spend up everything

Make yourself go insane
or shun yourself to uncharted margins
Make yourself smile, bloodlessly
Make me happy always
In me you find a madness of meaning

Just for once, baby,
conceptualize my greatness
For once and always, simple sweetie,
leave all deities other than me faithless
Just from now on and forever
admit you blunder
when you inhibit my plunder

Just because you're
descended from the dirty
give me your gullibility and money

Money, money, money
For me, for me, for me
Pay me, pay me, pay
or scream and scream and scream
and bleed and bleed and bleed
Suffer and let me hear it
That's the one and only
proper use for you
baby believer, if you're a true adherent

MARTYR

I used to say
whatever unfolds
know what you stand for
but nowadays disagreement
might mean death
if you dream of a tomorrow
I can't get on board with
I'll go to the rally and
shoot you in the head
He's tearing down our country
Gutting it of guardrails
He's slavering to stack government agencies
with loyalists that will never challenge his
abuses of power

He's racist and gaining momentum
with those he's racist against
I don't understand it
but it's the truth and it's sour

But should we make of him
a martyr no
That's a part he already hams up
Better to let him
admit his amorality
from time to time
while flying off at the gums
Pay attention when he keeps telling us
retribution's his game
but we mustn't let it be ours

We mustn't let him make
government a game
all about polishing his crown of stars

It doesn't exist
but his supporters swear they see it
He told them it would
blink into vision
if only they believe
They ate that shit up
Defecated then re-scarfed it
The MAGAs will storm
every center of influence
if you so much as kick out his feet

He is dangerous
Danger is not the remedy
even though he's trying to kill
the American dream with a surfeit
of misinformation and disinformation
and random outbursts of confession
about who he's targeting

We have to find ways to stop him
without being radicalized by his rhetoric
He likes to talk about
shooting someone on Fifth Ave
but all he better do is fantasize
Now that he's a felon de-gunned

Let's not level our own
Not stoop to the level of

dumbed-down violent madness
he wishes for us
He's victorious in political violence
which he'll surely profit from

He'll put his bloody rusted face
on mad kinds of merch
T-shirts and fannypacks
Hats and thermoses
Hoodies and the stained glass at church

Fire not at his bloviating foulness
and end up increasing his potency, potentially
His seepage's cold corruption
spreading exponentially

Because there's no reward
for gunning our shared American nightmare down
It just puts everything at risk
Democracy is the victim even if you miss

INNER BALDWIN

The queer interrogator
of outrageous fortune
asks the right questions
He says "Does this blessing bless
more than just me?"
Well, hell yes, actually
It was sent festooned and fierce
Friending him and finding his fault lines
In mere minutes he's mapped
Writing diatribes doubling as directions
He's got this idea James Baldwin
could jam bad to this
He'd be owned by awe for an audience
A proclaimer, a trouble-namer,
A tell-it-like-it-is-er
Baldwin ropes him in rapt
Reverbing revolutionary
Showing some things never change
Thereby changing everything
He didn't invent the art
of uncomfortable insight
He unencumbered it through innovation
He fired up the queer interrogator
with blistering indictment
of all that bleeds the nation
All that's wounded by willing it whiter
Now this white boy's fired by desire
to leverage any privilege placed on him
to dismantle privilege
Curating community of more colorful heritage

The interrogator asks his inner Baldwin
if it's ok for his paler kin to internalize
his drive for due justice
Inner Baldwin says with some irascibility
the genuine article would be
in no rush to trust us
An inner Baldwin rendered by this white boy
This white queer interrogator
but he'd work with
whatever works, he supposes
if Baldwin's spirit could have its say here
If he could bestow blessings
on anyone bothering
to be a bit better than bad history before
of his virtuoso verses imparted
to any color with ears to hear more

THE WORST ONE

Did he really win
the first time around
or did Russia help him rig it

Did he really score a
swing state blow-out
the third time around
or did his vote stealing
get more competent

Regardless
he's head of state again now
and we'll all have to try
to survive him

An aerial view of
the next four years
shows tanks in the streets
rolling over citizens
who all eventually end up
on the enemies list

A shroud enveloping
every square foot of America
Darkening our story

We'll stop telling kids
there are no monsters
We'll tell them "Be the worst one
and you won't have to worry about it"

This timeline might not
be salvageable
after the new/old president's
sickness thickens the smog

We'll go from
a nation of immigrants
to immigration being outlawed

Any struggles with
any dysphoria
might get you
singled out as a target
by Dear Leader's party

The swing voters swung
behind a man-shaped
mass of lies
because they find
authenticity alarming

METAPHYSICAL

87% OF THE TIME IN THE SIMULATION

When the mood strikes it's moon pulled
It is a veil whose wearer doesn't weep

When they build you a statue will you
come see it or would being photographed
in front of it thumbs-upping just be too much

If they step on your fingers when you're picking up
dropped pens and dropped whispers
tell them the monsters came for you and you're
getting along all right

If they cry when they know you're looking and
that makes you love them well then love them for it
Brief the guardian of your heart's gated secrets that
sometimes you find the rhyme that's welcome anytime

and when you find it you must tie it to
the sturdy chair of your aw shucks disenchantment
and it will tell you its truest tale or have to get through
one real bitch of a bad time

that stretches over and across the glitch in the picture of
the screensaver shoreline shown to the traumatized
intern you psychically linked with 87% of
the time in the simulation

in the backyard of tribulation you might find
amens still milling about their business kissing
blessings your best bet is believing the seed of
salvation still resides in

Still and always there slouches a shadow
stutters the gallery of ghosts I get good intel from

Hard pass on backrubs my mind's eye says
to them while right in front of me you're saying you love me
really you love me but just not like that

Maybe he's lying I think wildly graspingly
and maybe you are but even if so I won't know
unless I'm psychic like the little quiz online said I wasn't

If you know when it's done by pure instinct all the time you're
better at this than I

The end of one poem and start of another can be
such thin battle lines

SIGNALINGS

A flood of phraseology
fighting to become the first or last word
All night long, for mysterious reasons,
barking, growling dogs
All life has a right to its signalings
of satisfaction or dissatisfaction
The cat regards me coolly
his thoughts inscrutable as usual
It's up to me to find a place for this
This electric longing that lightnings my lassitude
I will nest it safely here
returning to visit at regular intervals
There's a distance only this closes
This process of mining kinds of landmines
Categorizing the mic drops and logic loops
and peaks of every trip
to bridge the gap between all that is
and all I know how to let in
Not to mention what I now know enough not to
Doors you can't lock until you stop
adjudicating their existence as debatable
There do exist primordial enemies
He is fact, the devil devouring
and fact, the doubtful still doubting
a loving God even as He saves them
from how many snapping jaws
so often they stop noticing
This is a place for showing I notice Him
in the protective growls of my dogs
who would defend me from any size devil

and the imperturbable nap of my cat's calm non-judgment
In the pull on my innards by the promise of blank paper
In omens daily, in reconciliation with kin
In longer, angrier hurricane seasons
In discovery of living doctrine

EDGEWISE

Nowadays everything's a struggle
Finding the dope or steering clear of the bubble

Making anyone happy
Especially myself
Remembering to eat or sleep or dream well

It's like a curse draped over me
A blanket that suffocates
That won't let me make
skin to skin contact with anyone

A voice that drones onward
through friction's heat or heart's drama
That won't let friends or lovers
get in anything edgewise

I swear it muffles everything
When I drown it
it resuscitates
I don't let it in so it harrows my outside
It wants deep entry
Wants to conquer and claim me
Sometimes denying it is all that calms me
in the midst of bullying blasphemy

No one else can hear it
when it bestows on itself Godhood
Declaring itself Almighty
when the God I know would never trip like this

I take my medicine
to defang it and garble it
Close it up behind heavy curtains
of steely soundproof somnambulance

Leaves me in a fog that never quite lifts
A precarious predicament
It wrecks with indica's effect
Times ten thousand
Plus bewilderment

So don't expect me to pick up
every social cue
I miss the mad rush to pay the check
Flummox the furtive flirt
Only capable of checkering
in games of mental chess

I forget where I'm expected
Fall asleep when I'm the watchman
Ask for explanations when it's all my idea
Flaming out as barely a flicker
Fresh out of everything but flop sweat

It's the mouth or the bad head weather
It's give it your ear or give up your sight

It's all on me and the true Godhead I harry
to judge me mercifully when grace joins the fight

FINAL SHRINE

All time is all happening at once

Our attention paid gives the world its shape

One final shrine this quarter moon

gives the invocation appropriate weight

Every session I sharpen knives against trauma

My shielding shed, traded for nerve

Ninety appointments with one hundred questions, pointed

right at what hurts

What must be unlearned

Every pill I dose myself with on schedule

Trying to reach sobriety's pinnacle

Six prescriptions for seven diagnoses

I knock 'em back but I don't expect miracles

ONLY THE UNDERTOW

At water's edge, scrabbling up on a pier
Surrounded by an insectoid, homopterous buzzing
Watching turtles bob on the surface
Daring then shying
Such simmering heat, even
my shadow's flash-frying

Brain aloft in my imaginarium, I'm building
with all bells and whistles
monuments to apocrypha
while dipping a toe in
Given to hoping the turtles aren't snappy
or the moccasins ornery
but nature feeds all beasts, I guess
To every bite and sting, an ordering

Tempting pleasure teases torment
but look at the fusillade of colors
a panoramic sky can implement
Purple hues and spectrum of orange
Bird egg blue and burnished bronze
Here, hovering near, as though it
cares to come and witness me
To idiot-proof my search for God's brushwork
Anyone who won't see it
forever lives in my sympathies

I stay 'til sunset slips through satin
of another evening's curtain
Knowing very little
but a few things for certain

Sight is pure miracle
Sound to accompany, deft magic
Life paints with a lush palette
on ephemeral canvas
Still waters move me
with the multitudes they contain
but the sky's so deep tonight
only the undertow knows my fate

I'M LOST IF YOU'RE LOST

We can't let Heaven get crowded

That thought process, I can't respect
That's a faith so depraved
sharing's no longer an option
Convinced that God would allow a few of us
to hog every molecule of His devotion

To help all stand together
all together should bend
Mercy's hymn is for her and for him,
For they/them and the gender continuum,
All embody amen

About time to stop
leaving the siblings behind
who slip off the sides
of rigid paths in narcissistic paradigms

I'm saved if you are
I'm lost if you're lost to me
I'm serious but hopefully not heavy handed
Our bandwidth is buoyant abundance
to nourish your peace
Not threaten you into belief

We can't leave the devil
with no one to supervise

That thought process, what soul can survive
About time to start honoring God's art
You think you're not a masterpiece
just because you're missing some teeth
and being shrugged off as sinful
makes your heavy heart mean

But appraisal in the abstract
doesn't do your realism justice
It insults intrinsic integrity

When everyone's a critic
nobody trusts us

All your infractions, momentary lapses
Some recurring somewhat intentionally
Not a one recurring eternally

In what version of justice
would God shun sons and daughters
of his own craftsmanship
for an endless infernal sentence
of parental neglect and abandonment

I'm damned if you are
Any of us is worth going after
Worth saving even from the sewer
Love begrudges neither
the broken or the bastard

If the pearly gates are high up
it's right to keep reaching down

We all sing the song or
the choir's unsound

In any version of omnipotence
Salvation has to be omnipresent
since no kingdom could be perfect or glorious
without all our ancestors and descendants

You think we presume to save you
Truth is, we can't save anyone without you
If you're condemned, I have no defense
You'd be right to doubt God
if God were to doubt you

SHRUG

Aggressive
in sin and repentance
I'm making the mistakes I need to
Transgressive
Digging my grave
Hyperstimulation
Smooth as glass
most every time I smoke with you

I'm so full of shit
It's truth you spit
I'm a hypocrite
It's your duty to report it

Vindictive
and most all you've known is violence
Hungry violence
Vengeful hunger
Best move on
before I test your toothsomeness

You're so full of grit
I'm all aphasia and malaise
You're accidentally brilliant
I'm only ever smart on purpose
You got it all
and think nothing of it
I got a ghost of a chance
and damn well better love it
Your sidestep instinctual

My cockeyed optimism
barely tempers curses
You pay zero dollars
but can't be bothered
I go broke and swear somehow it's worth it

Inventive
My layered lies get so inventive
but I get so exhausted
earning all invectives
I glimpse what's becoming of the real me
and I do the full soul freak

I'm not a Gemini but I should've been
Your detached gutting of goldmines
is impressively consistent
I'm not about to stand for
any ransoming of secrets
You smile with no trace of humor
Shrug and say *then sit*

AND

Morning light and blinding glare

First kiss and last laugh

Foggy gloom and heavy air

Caffeine jitters and sugar crash

Making it matter and calling it off

Writing it down and making your mark

Sampling the dish and settling for the trough

Shrouding the truth and laying it stark

What you won't believe and what you can't say

The safety of your bed and the danger of his

How far you'll go and where you choose to stay

Your last chance shot and the odds that you'll miss

A glitch in the framework and a compulsion in your system

An imperative to move and a cause to stand firm

A place outside time and an end to earthly bedlam

A host of sins forgiven and mercy undeserved

GONE

You can have my
verse but can't
hold it like it held me
Like a doting mother
existing for her offspring

You're also poet-souled
Fear and fantasy flotsamed
within the futility

A hemisphere of scorched earth
masquerading as man
As individual, as working class cog

Have you noticed your paycheck
just says "All gone"

Even if it said "Here, have this nine
with unlimited zeroes trailing after"
You'd doubtless keep on doing this
Craning up at constellations

You can vigil with me any old time
Where any young peace awaits affixing
to any watchful wish silently wailed for

Can't chart its course by the stars
Just a stray scrap of feeling
to suggest the magic's working

Then you clap your big hands
while I emit a small hum
Will this harmony last
I will it to, but it's gone

Sitting duck meets sitting duck
The void chewing the antithesis
where once was a world

Your world crowning mine
My world losing atmosphere reaching
your unself-conscious elevations

Incinerating with us
folded space crumples
Crinkles in on rending reality
No more dry or deadpan
clever turns of phrase
No more gallows humor
No more time anyplace

Wait though, one
Then two pulses pulse
Strumming strong
Sound itself may be deleted
but sing it, son
The hopeless rock on

I've decided to throw you a party
Let you protest that it's not even your birthday
while I present you with this conflicted mess
"Is it all too much or is it all gone?"
I'll demand
"You're in this so make it make sense."

I STRIVE

I'm lost again, please find me, Father

Tempest tossed again, made brittle by autumn

I feel so fated always to falter

Never to finish my God given project

Still I strive and plead for help

to harvest stories I'm needed to tell

Knowing Heaven's love after loving all Hell

INTERSECTIONS

Another summoning
to pray on paper
The easy ink flow
a tithe to divine nature
Another call goes out
or perhaps it's all the same call
that never stops
My better angels find me here
at another dawn
filtering forces best not fought

Few flowers still stand up to wintry fall
No birds singing except in the south
Somber skies, skeletal trees
Ghost energies I can't quite cast out

Should I befriend the phenomena
Am I certain I'm entirely unhexed
What breaks through
to haunt this bender I'm on
Bloodless be the banishment

Unpoisoned if at all possible
Sent away without scent of sage
Warded off without
wounding their ectoplasm
Translocated to someplace
wraiths can be safe

A deer walks right up
to my doorstep
Another summoning
by some soundless signal
Looks at me for a long time
through the window
like it knows something
I don't know

Share the secret, I beseech
Sacred soul, communicate your piece

Do you see
someone else but me

What's the origin
of the entity

Oh choir coalesce around me
Divinity defend
intersections irrevocably
opened in me
My perimeter needs securing again

DID THIS TO YOURSELF

What do you say we split the difference
or spin your rolodex of random excuses

If you got the means you will be ended
Oh learn how to fuck off

You did this to yourself
No one else's fault
Have a care which God you exalt

It's like you forgot your untied head
But I summon smiles, patient with your dissonance

All at once it all finishes falling apart
Hysterics won't help us
Please no histrionics
Oh learn how to fuck off if you
won't learn how to listen
Dumbass too snobby
for divine intervention

Is your cross too heavy
Are you too lazy

It's like you forgot your meaning and footing
You won't cure that with the smoke
of foggy memory
We're bound in forms corporeal
Easily distracted, easy to kill

Mangled by the matrix
Every agony sure feels real

THE SPIRIT MOVES

There on the wall
Do you see
the eye of God
peering out from the light scatter
filtering up the stairs and
over the banister
A visitation rolling in
from a partitioned off room

All I know is in here
the spirit moves
God eye tracking me, dilating
wincing at my repetition
of petered out plotlines

Set right by His sight
by His design
His device is all that anything
ultimately is of mine
Learning to operate
grace God given

Easing into blessing
Easing out of hard living

He manifests for us
He declines to hide His glorious face
We're comprised of filthy rags
We're trashed but He stays

See His face not looking away
Get ok with meeting His gaze

Be sorry bruh
but don't *just* be sorry
Pitch new twists
Steer the story
towards the blood
that always saves you
while you pray for the day
you wake up sin-proof

VEILS

Just breathe and be at peace with your beliefs
Let your rivals run with you and be not enemies

Don't demand from your deity
an elaborate standard of care
Be content with basics like fresh water and air

Know that few things are certain and
not everything's eventual
You can rest on your laurels and you
might still luck into your potential
You can attain expertise and hone your body
and train your mind
and all your focus might not get you
to the strived-for summit alive

Still, lounging loses its luster
when losing the plot gets lonely
Learn about all you can firsthand
but remember it all amounts to only
the culmination of your experiences
thus far on planes we can
only see in three dimensions
There's more to life behind more veils
than we're accustomed to sensing

But what communion might we be capable of
if we don't greet the implication
of impossibility with undue deference
If the potential threat level isn't
our only existential frame of reference

We have all this wiring and the fact is
we don't know what all we're wired for
so don't just assume
you can't surprise yourself anymore

Stretch your soul's senses like
intuition and instinct are limbs
Be assured that you are spirit and
spirit animates flesh
Our current vessels might not be our first or best

Ask yourself what else we can hotwire the ignition to
What wild rides we might catch to what realms
Quantum physics allows for boundless energies
filling up every gap in every particle of ourselves

Every particle of everything we observe
Undetectable but indispensable
Unknowable forces permeate our whole world

Don't settle for that state of affairs
Seek to know especially when the science says *no*
Evolution leaps
Capacities advance
Ride the slingshot effect when your mind gets blown

Get lost sometimes in places
your essence might remember originating from
There's less we can access than what we know
Less we see than what we're shown

Make friends with mystery
because there's always another one
Don't ever think you've mapped
how far the rabbit hole goes

SECRET KNOWLEDGE

Who can tell in what fever dream
we can learn secret knowledge
Where we might be ushered into catacombs
by night's veil parting
Catacombs parallel to here but
out of step with our physics
A venue with advantages both
for hiding and detecting what's hidden

Who knows what states of being
entities made of cosmic particles can achieve
What resonances we might answer instinctively
What liminal spaces we might cocoon in
Our lineage's comprehensive inheritance
In thick air, broad daylight, a spectral
curtain roped open

THE BACK FOOT

Thought I had to fend for myself
Hide my dust jacket so my title's
a little harder to tell
because people think they already know
every scene of every story told

But maybe we're quick to pick up
all each other's tricks now
It takes two for every time
to hit like bricks now
Could've gotten it right
Gave me something to write

I just gotta learn to appreciate
when God gives out gifts
I'm not talking about you but
the kind of thing that really sticks to the ribs
I might be a mongrel
Please educate me on what mercy is
Fending for myself only gets me good riddance

Too easy to find yourself
broken spirited on the back foot
Too easy to misalign yourself
Suddenly you're banging heads with the bad hoods

But parties with people
never fail to go pear shaped
So when you party you don't even
invite anyone these days

Yet you're compelling reason to fight
You and me getting good together
Better futures at each other's sides
The devil's been my downfall
but I'm sick of being lured by the lies
We're not already lost
We're adrift but light keeps us alive

ZOMBIED

What kind of child have I been?

What man, what powers, can name signify?

Where, with what weapon, blessed by Heaven?

Recall the times "I repent!" I cried

Entreat on repeat, holler for the holy

Head on swivel, zombied, to excess driven

My prayer is always a higher mission

DELIVER ME

Gratitude for graying hands
with the power of multitudes
of angels in their wrath

Wrath against the original enemy
Quick on their wings
from whom to deliver me

Gratitude for spoken tongues
never known by me or
perhaps by anyone
with meaning well taken
and understood

The Prince of Peace is alive
The God of Love is good

Gratitude for clarity returning
for peace of mind forever burnished

Can't thank God enough
but I'll sure try

The purpose in adversity
today was realized

LIFEBREATH

Blood spills sacrificed to rebirth

A splotchy red rose blooming

as though painted by gory brush

Openly discarded evidence

Now the hieroglyphs

of redemption's entreaty are rendered

Surrendered power to the lifebreath of all power

I scale sky tops singing for transcendence

Tucking and rolling to cut through turbulence

above the alpenglow of home

Extending a hand to meet happy-go-lucky eternity

I've been finding real gems

refracting rhythms of prayerful refrains

Crimson emerald amber auras

Light pouring from love's embodiment blue

Yes said to Yahweh

the stasher and scatterer of gems

We thrum through space to one another

disappointing meaning's void

THE ETHER

Alert again, I don't dwindle, I kindle

Rested up, in love with my lyrics

Torn down, so much in my blood

Setting my splint, rousing my spirits

Others too, larking at my same level

Singing out, synced decibel by ragged decibel

Accept the ether, learn, never fear this

A FEATURE AND A BUG

Care to embrace the most
elongated endeavor ever

No training wheels on the pens
people just let me have
Almost like I'm considered an adult now

A mature mammalian specimen
Poet caste, pops off at the mouth to
earn almost no money

Both a feature and a bug, perhaps
He digs getting deep but sometimes
he lands on funny

Slipping into third person and
right back out with
reckless, senseless abandon
In poetry, anything can be anything
It's only really resonant
if you don't understand it

I just turn it on like a hose
So enigmatic
So damn emblematic
A real slice of life
of America at large
Gayed up, of course
because now I'm in charge

Sure you're secure in your masculinity or
your soccer mom sensibilities
but within you winnows growing alarm

They let him have pens
Now his arsenal's armed

He is me, but I hover, at times
a little outside my body
like I'm but an observer of
a mad motherfucker
An emissary of a
magnificent mouthpiece

We're both allowed to use pens
Without guardrails, gayly
You're not promised
straight streets or safety

All roads wind within and if you're
honest you're kinda liking it
Cruising in a convertible of id
Breathing hard even though
it's a sin
What color is your psycho-mobile
Mine's every blue ever invented
all at once

Both fire and ice
can be blue, realize
Am I making you sweat
or shivering you inside

Play for keeps or play nice
Reel in the riot or desire the fight
I won't be about acrimony but
I might be up in arms when I'm right

It's my standards, out-singing slander
Dangerously dexterous, nearly untied
My wild rhythm's been all
bound up in rallying cries
for my malnourished aspects

The child never allowed
to hit back
or cry himself out
with necessary intensity
The delinquent, always missing or mouthy
The punching bag, empathizing with attackers
deciding he deserved it

The common denominator that
strings my selves together
is every me I'll ever be will have courage

My psyche's known for spiking
'til the Richter Scale reads me
but I forge ahead, I mean, I forge a
whole new head

One that doesn't stress making sense
with the wrong ingredients

Placid madness from scratch, raving sanity
under the lash
These are what make up my peaks
and valleys and plateaus
but locked away in my recesses
I still remember everything I
wish I didn't know
The story arc ain't really about anything
as much as it's about everyone
I hate even entertaining it sometimes
but that's who we're called to love

Someone's gotta make it weird
Someone's gonna striptease dropping their guard
Not me, though, even my skin is a barricade
I'm a murder machine
A circling shark
I'm every weapon designed for doomsday
I'm poison-tipped and sharp

Just trust it, never test it
It's only phantom pains where I
used to keep my heart

Reach for me, reach me
I can't be reached
That wasn't me asking, telepathically
A hand to hold isn't
an actual need
You don't die without it
Well, you do, you die regardless

The point is, I don't dream of soft things
I wouldn't let your arms equal armistice
I don't look for you every time I go out
I'd never plant you a garden
I never expend energy on sestinas you won't see

They don't exist, I say
and I hate you anyway

I turn it on like a hose
Like a big fire hose
to flood out sentimentality with vitriol
I won't be in love, I prefer other drugs
I don't waste time wishing
you thought I was wonderful

I don't think you're amazing or anything
and if I did, thinking it wouldn't
make me even madder
I'm not just some dude, no, I'm
the shadow of doom
I'm lethal and I kill without blinking
except not right now, maybe
'cos my eyes keep leaking

Tissues for issues
Totems for touchstones
An hourglass resentment might shatter
Begrudging falling sands that ruin plans
I'm not killing time 'cos I want it to suffer

I didn't start this
Time said it would heal me but
it just aged me
Time's the party always
breaking its promise

It never tries to save us
It feeds on and fades us

Man, I tried to be sweet to it
Then I tried for an amicable split
but it still runs its fingers all over me
Runs them through my hair
making it disappear

It won't honor restraining orders
It's flat out unreasonable
Just a sociopathic tyrant on a tear
'til it runs out on unseized potential
Unmade epiphanies
Unobserved altars

Sometimes I still thirst for magic
when strict adherence falters

Sometimes the soul of me thinks it
knows spellcraft and Tarot is of God
I might revive a ritual but first
I always read Psalms

Prayer is power
Tragedy is a tower
No one is nowhere
Don't give up, I'm still in here
Climbing back in my body
Baptized and brainy
Scarred and sarcastic
A formidable entity
Making no move towards escaping
This time every shade's staying

No distancing in third person this time
The rift was getting real but I
remain Travis Prime

Reconciled, newly attuned
An equilibrium I mustn't
let mindflayers ruin

Meat hooks in your astral body
Lay you out, leave you so dotty
Crush through the crust of
your subconscious repressions
Twist your secret soul musculature
into ghastly positions

You can't let them in, can't rock
with their rhythm
Can't make the mistake just to
extract the wisdom
That priceless pearl or needed nuglet
from getting caught deep in dumb shit

Be smarter for once
before everything hurts worse
Before you have to bribe officials
with pucker and purse
Before nothing is sacred
notice all of it is
That's why, eventually, all of us
take someone's shit

We take it from somebody
or a string, or a genus of somebodies
because we saw through someone's eyes
much like theirs once
and the view, for a stretch
was singularly lovely
Because their hidden, ferreting hurt
tenderized some empathy trauma
tucked into us

Because other cheek turning is reflexive
once we glimpse how beautiful
anyone once was

He doesn't mean what he's saying right now
He's first-person thriced again until he calms down
Mindflayer, nonesuch, no, but he's
laid to nappy by the mind*nanny*
'til he stops his awkward undulations
in the general direction of romance

Actually, I mean what I say most times
even when I do what I said I wouldn't
Like letting the flayers boss me around
after I rewrote myself so strong they couldn't

But let me tell you something else
Angels make meaning from lack
Hell's for wealth
So lock onto that sacred aspect
of every last thing
Heaven lets you keep
for even half the duration of
your apportioned century

The important stuff we reunite with
when vitals fail
and mercy becomes forgiveness
and forgiveness ferries us home

'til then many of us
spruce up shanties
out of whatever we can on the road
Mourning much and much alone

Many of us mangle what means the most
and accrue a few keepsakes it hurts
each time we look at
but we carry them along to
wonder at anyway
In any dim light, baubles unwrapped

But to every night a day
To every roadblock, an alternate route
To every longing, a quietening
To every screaming agony
one that renders us mute

Gets so a good time is one
that doesn't remind of anyone, anywhere
even though we know they're still in here
More real, maybe, than we are
we mangy mummudrai of memories
Of slang that haunts us when spoken
because we first heard the phraseology
from a lover who wasn't done
loving others when we landed them
or an enemy we didn't have to cripple
A mother we didn't make it
to the death bed of
Compatriots already gone or terminal

This is why, we think, he reverts
so often to humor
It helps him to alleviate
tragedy's many contusions
but pens allowed to lark
will also look
at what the hoped for laughter
hopes to cover
A hose turns off, too
Thins to a trickle the
madness that mutters
The *ha ha* that deflects
The suggestive aside that affronts

'til it's just me again
making the most of the
emotions that have me for lunch

ROUGH WEATHER PRAYER

Home safe thanks to God's grace
Drove right through the storm
Freezing rain, a heart that stays warm
Killed my last pack of cigarettes
I'll save some money to pay back my debts
'cos today I'm moved by some immutable spirit
I promise if it stays with me I'll always endeavor to hear it
The words are coming easy again
like they do when divinity and I are friends
I've no appetite for a fight with what's right
I still got love for God's night but I remember God is light
Light is my burden 'cos it's not me who lifts it
Anywhere is home when you're forever a misfit
so I'm safe in my house and safe on the road
Safe in rough weather and safe in harbored hope
I'll take my hits and nurse my damage
Vengeance ain't mine, it's my Creator's to manage
I'll stay awake today or catch up on sleep
Either way I'm His to keep

LET IT GO

Duality is a one man show
performed tonight at the end of my rope

What if I just let it go
My eyes on skies calling me home

I can't sleep, I can't wake up
It's in my head, it's in my blood

Dull roar, heavy pressure, maddening love
If I was smart, I'd cut and run

It's like the romance to a cigarette
The appeal of the precipice

Carefully administering the trip
Flirting with falling off a cliff

Part of me is curled up fetal
Part of me longs for the needle

The part that's fond of whatever's fatal
I hold in stasis the best I'm able

CARRYING THE STONE

Smoked so much it made me sick
Strangled a newborn poem in the crib
I've closed up shop for the rest of the day
Maybe the week, the way I feel at this rate

I've gotta take better care of myself
The routine rhyme scheme becomes a death knell
to what I really have a deep need to say
Maybe I'll sleep instead
Flattened by chest pains

Humbled by a headache
before I can peel back the layers
of any dark inclinations or urgent prayers

It's no use
It's gotten obtuse
Still veering into verse even though
I'm getting worse
Lighting up another
Coloring my drawn face grayer
Hunched over hocking up lung matter

Words lie in wait to assault and batter
Beat a confessional piece out of me
Curl me up on the floor as candor just bleeds

I told poetry no
Now no is becoming the poem
Such a surprise to catch myself carrying the stone

Rolling uphill boulders of brevity and levity
A Sisyphean task
All hopes of rest and recuperation dashed

I'm hungry and tired
The next verse is starving for me
and staring saucer eyed alert
Making my nerves misfire
Peace of mind goes unprioritized

The holistic view that I've done enough
won't hold up
Can't shut off my stuff
It comes to claim me no matter how I protest
Clamping down like cardiac arrest

It's never finished
even when I tell it not to start
My willpower taffy
more smoke pulls apart

Lights my brain on fire
Fuses my spine to my chair
Sets my pen song scrying
Lays the brutal truth bare
That I'm not going anywhere
'til the riled rhythm rattling
my bones becomes aware

And breaks loose from me
A living thing
I'll sacrifice my sleep to its slithering

AMERICAN ENTROPY

I'm out of sorts
but my own help's better than yours
I have years on you
and more mileage than you assume
I'm capable of grander passion and deeper apathy
in fluctuations faster and more erratic
than your dire dreams or high hopes
could keep pace with

You don't want to understand
anymore than I want to explain it

So I shamble away from you
Shirk the horny hood-rat scene
Part the swollen sea of skanks writhing
to the beat of creative bankruptcy
The cadence of American entropy

I'm the island our indoctrination
insists no one can be
I existed before you walked on me
I trip over no trophy or touch

I do not need to be happy

I make haste for no race
Prowl for no play
Zero isn't a number
It is a state of grace

SUNKEN

What adversity made of what substance
What percentage opportunism and emptiness
How malleable malfeasance
What level of atrocity have we learned to find acceptable
This is a whole new border-blocked no man's land
and especially no woman's
who isn't knocked up or soon to be
Birthing blessings of rapist reflections
Bearing life even if it's a death sentence
Bundles of like-it-or-not bloody joys
for autopiloted fertile toys
Virile victimizers attacking brains like vapors
Trembling terrors turn to torpor
Modern America is decidedly dark age
Always nice to put namelessness
to a shock-sunken face
Trauma is a tide that needs no reason why
Clench now and spawn without assistance of midwife
Rinse and repeat, perpetual birthing, big bleed
It's all such a good show for redneck assemblages
Pageantry of greed inbreeds
A contest that kills and calls dying the prize
Reality conforming to trumpier and trumpier lies
How howling mad to think this wholesome
How horror-tinged
How hued by Hell
Lady Liberty mad mobbed and violated where she fell
Now each and every one of us
might as well be the trailer park tankhead
toppling over into NASCAR neo Nazi deathbed

Priding in our profound purpose
of plain as day persecution
Every sicko sicced on a minority
A shining soldier saluted
Best our broken shards not bother
asking what it says about any of us
that we watched patriotism's poisoned pyre
and didn't try to be antidotes hard enough
It's the darkest timeline inescapable
It's the fascist kind of fucked
Freedom is for insurrectionists and their president
bashing journalist heads and spilling activist guts
The laugh track is automatic
It's what the autocrat and his billionaire henchman expect of us
Sharing laughter at unshared sacrifice
Corpses never stack high enough

WORDLESSLY

We're all the life of the party tonight
Rocking our individual cones of silence
I keep trying to start conversations
Employing anecdotes and wryness

Like it's a contest they'll lose
by taking the bait
The other cats here
are too smooth to play
with the dangled string of
"Guess what happened when…"
or the jangly mouse of
"Nice hands, feet!"

I barely recall us boisterous now
Just well enough to miss us terribly

Something's downing us
Weighing us
Multiplying our gravity
I ask if you're ok
You say, "Not really"
but won't elaborate

So I say
"Yeah me either"
Try to say more but
my vocabulary's enfeebled
by some shapeless overbearance
Some oppressive omnipresence
But I don't need the right words
By now prayer's in my reflexes

Flares fired off
to a listening benevolence
to reopen cauterized channels
Circumvent this lingual helplessness

Just something that settled over us
Some form of shuffling sleep
we sink further into
when we try to verbalize

This is how brethren break ranks
How we lose the bonds we
forget how to fortify
Unless we wordlessly unify
Finding love in brothers personified

CRY DARKLING

Come out and play
Bury your gays
Be sore afraid
even on your best days

Go to ground
Don't be seen around town
Heart be stout
but some things aren't allowed

Make mince meat
of urchins from the street
Their minds break so easily
Exploitation is a breeze

Cry wolf cry tiger cry darkling
Prone in the pitch's pit sparkling
Ices your veins hearing hellhounds barking
Your brain's a mainframe fritzing and sparking

Steamroll the protesters vengefully
Eat the endorphin rush effortlessly
Trending totals sums automatically
Goon to the mad militia's flattery

Intimidate immigrants daily
Say they kidnapped a dozen dogs and ate them
Pretend chicken is cats they're filleting
Your echo chamber's acoustics are amazing

Retrace the twisted turn
Get us back to some moral to learn
A bad example is a bad reputation earned
Amp divine awe for faith to affirm

WITHOUT

Gutted for the greater good
Iron-eyed under pulled down hood

I will write about this and make it ok
Reveal what I can learn from this latest pain

How I wouldn't be me without it
How it's formative and all for the best
I will make myself believe it
No force will make me confess

That it's killing me to pay this cost
Ending me to absorb this loss
Rupturing me to go without
Ruining everything and I'm done for now

HORROR SHOW

My fevered aspirations
for what a poem can do are lofty
I'd rather aim too high
than slither on my belly too low
but the day gets away from me
with a scarcity of stanzas born whole

Partial delivery of kicking legs or twisted torso
A dismembered terror; just poetry's loose bones

Are those words that unformed mouth is mewling
We may never know
The meter goes into shock
The incubated ballad's broke
The lump of a face, spectral blue
The balled little fist, gravemoss cold

I don't put these tragic fragments out of their misery
Don't scoop these sad segments into the disposal
Don't cluck my tongue and dress the shreds down
No, I overcome my initial disapproval

These unattached extremities, dislodged from sockets
Never tightened or trued
Though lamentable, might be plantable
Might push up from the soil
Unfolding eerie but exquisite blooms
Sometimes even slices of poem form can surprise you
by growing back the trunk torn or limbs left off
Crawling after their mesmerized poet parent

Who can't bring themselves to leave a
single line of their lyrical lineage to rot
No matter its humble horror show origin
No matter if almost all of it is anatomically incorrect
That it squirms from its amniotic sac just to
topple on its misshapen head

I just wanted to have my say
Just wanted to say something universal
Something profound and incisive
Transgressive for noble objective
Fit for nudging mountains
whispers of inches in progressive directions
Wanted to drill down on some weighty dialogue
worthy of man and God's attention

What I got is something else altogether
Something less than the sum of its tortured parts
A malformation maladjusted
Slouching sickly into my heart

MENTICIDE

Where do I go, what should I do
when my whole world fails
to offer anything new
to examine through poetry's lens
or fashion myself after, in tribute to
When the fact my lines keep stumbling over
is I'm simply still not over you

Still not even close, to be real
Still hiding from fault lines you laid bare
Sometimes I feel like I made you up
Were you ever really there

Was there a time you stood beside me
Defended me to bullies
Was that just the Mandela Effect
Would another me from
elsewhere in the multiverse
remember the whole thing differently

It's more likely you annihilating me
is a multiversal constant
You stealing my confidence is
a key point of interdimensional convergence
Were you only ever sent to me
to make me doubt my discernment

What do I take with me, who do I turn to
when anything of value might
make me your target

and few would believe me about
menticide I can't prove
except by pointing to my skull
and begging my brainpan
to pick up and amplify
my boiling blood's outraged wail

I have no evidence of you
rolling off the rails
No corroborating witness to
you skipping merrily beyond the pale

Still not sure I remember it right myself
Looking myself in mirrors, mouthing things like
"This happened *to* you, not *because* of you"
My mind doesn't want to rehash the horror
It doesn't trust me or you to tell the whole truth

Is there a rock bottom below rock bottom
Do you haunt it from above or adjacent
From parallel to or passing through
In what obscure outcropping
are you stealthily stationed

It's a likely story that you've forgotten me
A lovely thought that you've ever forgiven
a single person who even tried
to redefine themselves
after becoming your victim

Your supply, for a time, on your side
Against ourselves, even, against all good reason

or instinct for self-preservation
I found others who
filled that role before me
and their attempts at recollection
left them similarly vacant
How can I stop you
does it ever end
To even your flickering image
burned behind my eyelids
will I always be the one who relents

UPWARD MOBILITY

I'm sick of feeling
like I can't have it
Like I'll never be it
Like I'm too damaged
So what if my
upward mobility is mauled
and my dreams are all savaged
Give me what I'm after
Satiate my avarice

YESTERDAY REPEATING

Everyone leaves, memories remain.
Pray for amnesia to kill my pain.

Lies behind my back.
Lies to my face.
I'm not perfect.
I guess I'm to blame.

No one knows me.
No one ever has.
I gave me away.
I'll never get me back.

I gave me away.
I was stolen.
Every day, I die in slow motion.
Every night, I lie and I know it.

I say it's ok, I say it will be,
but tomorrow is always
yesterday repeating.

JUST

Some kind of preprogrammed machine
to do these small, repetitive things
Not be a song summoner
Not a lyric lassoer
Just a pleasure chaser
Just a feeder and a hungerer

Some rope-a-dope business plan
to yank my guts out as performance art
Now you're all trauma tourists
Now I'm a bleeder for every reader
Just a percussionist on fallen horse flesh
Just a cataloguer of curses

Some manner of technological pet trained
to listen with all the wetware of my human vessel
Taught to fetch and roll over
Taught to congratulate and capitulate
Just a conversation piece following you place to place
Just for your feet, my soft, round face

Some whack-a-mole recidivism
to keep my recovery on track for tomorrow
Conned by myself into romanticizing relapse
Conned by my buttoned up besties into sobriety relentless
Just a torture trick to keep me white knuckling
Just deleting my history 'cos I've had enough of me

MOVING IN

Tonight I seem to need all the medicine
Wonder if I'll ever feel well again
Hard to believe tomorrow will bring new experience
I fight the despair but sometimes it wins

It bubbles over onto the page
even when it's not what I want to write
because saying anything else would
feel like blatant lies

"Don't visit anymore," I tell it
"Be gone from my sight"

"Oh, I'm not visiting"
comes its stentorian reply
"I'm moving in to stay"
"All of you is mine"

I roll over in bed and my joints pop
I fluff my pillow but it stays limp
I try to sleep and starbursts of pain
go off in my dazed vision

Agony at the crossroads of body and spirit
Hurt a religion beating me into adherence
Life should never just be something to suffer
There's surely a lesson in this somewhere
Buried truth to make me tougher

But right now
whatever it might be is lost on me
Right now it feels like
punishment in perpetuity
for trying to love again
For a night spent watering optimism's seed
For trying to be anything but a yawning pit of need

NOTHING LEFT

There's nothing left of me
It all blew away
The mood stabilizers scrubbed every trace
I've fallen far and ditched myself
where outcries don't echo
I'm not even blue that my therapist is yellow
Stopped answering my calls
Skipped town and state and maybe country
I don't get disappointed
I'm gone so life can't punish me
I'm a blank drawn, a gap in memory
A note dropped and in fact
ending all involvement with music
I'm not alive enough to be considered artificial
Sleep of death forever is a damn sight better
than waking up wounded
No more neuroses to be shrunk
My trauma response has gone tepid
Soon my non-reaction to stimulus
will be wholesale, system wide
There's no reason to protect me from the truth now
People think I've lost my mind
but in truth I've popped my top
I'm not even inside

FORGETTING

Punishing peace and quiet
when I need raucous friends
Need bass booming sativa blunt rides
so my young heart can resurrect

What even is the point of me anymore
if I just keep forgetting I know that answer
I've felt that link established
Coalesced into cosmic cohesion

The snag is the coming back
Is all of me home again
What me am I mourning
The geography of this grief
is something none of me can name

MISCHIEF

Gotta cry as daylight dies
As night spills ink across the horizon
The evening is cold and bleak
Autumn brings endings but I don't oblige them
Fuck ups can be fortuitous, I reckon as I
big brother myself
They can also be gratuitous
To err is human but I should
at least share the wealth
Nothing about this date on the calendar
heralds a holiday or summons a sea change
Morose and minus mirth
Can't stay sane without getting strange
Nobody understands that I saw all this coming
I was pelted by portents
I heard marchers drumming
and still the blasphemous blare
caught me somewhat unaware
I swear I was watching but
every earthly pain still got me
But anyway
there's always a drug
A pill or a tonic
A prescription or a plug
A mind eraser or easer for a bad guy beleaguered
Make no mistake
I'm hardly the hero of my own story
I'm a piss poor protagonist
when the right thing is boring
Still I try to hold myself to a simple standard

I got my good humor and
I'm mostly well-mannered
Well-intentioned for the most part
'til mischief makes off with my mind
Gets me limber and loosened up enough
to dance with all the trouble I can find
Let it dip and twirl me
Get me dosed and dizzy
Letting myself love it
Letting love kill me
"Ask not who it tolls for"
"Remember it's for thee"
'til then I'll revel in any problems I please

SCREENS

All of us together
Isolated in our own little worlds
Stuck in our phones
Sparing each other few words
I fucking hate it if I'm honest
even though I'm as much
a part of it as anyone
Without these screens
thrown up between us
What do we fear we'd become
A little more there for each other
More prone to looking
people in their eyes
More attentive to what another person
is saying and not saying
Will anything ever bridge this divide
Does anyone else even want it to
or are these technologies that
make it easier to connect
only suited for pushing us further apart
To look at our heavily filtered social media
you'd never know what's happened
to the collective human heart
You'd never know any of us
are missing anything
Never know I just
ache and yearn all the time
but maybe you don't want to
Maybe I should post some idyllic lie
Maybe we can text each other
from the same room
but will we bother to reply

DONE TO DEATH

Reaching out, trying to connect to something
bigger than me, intangible, invisible
A link established before that has
sometimes let me down lately
Abandoning me to my own borders and limitations
A river that becomes a barrier
A silence that says nothing about anything

Making due, mining myself for inspiration
Foraging for verses and finding mostly vexation
An instinct to repeat what's already expressed
An undertow to struggle against
Grabbing at my panicked thrash
Reeking of unproductive rerun
Déjà vu done to death

Crashing out, giving up for now
on excavating nuance
or serving some shouting skydaddy's
searing mission statement
Sinking into soft sleep
A shushing of the screed from the deep
An insulation of blank dreamless peace

FRANKLY

Frankly his whole brain's bizarre
What it brings to light should stay in the dark
I wouldn't recommend wading in
unless you're a decorated psychiatrist
or he'll make you question if sanity itself
can possibly survive this
You'll come out of the collection cackling
and pitching a crying fit
You'll blunder around abstractly bowlegged
Your abstract orifices ripped
from letting his worrisome word
have its way with you
Granting him free reign to have
his fucked up fun
You won't believe in agency for artists
beyond PG-13
by the time his violence against
wholesomeness is done
Every subject matter mutates
Every tender turn of phrase
seems to bring an equal and opposite
degenerate shriek
He parades about and whips his monsters
He airs out their festering
like that's worthy of a witnessing too
as much as the next guy's
sweet heart swelling swoons
dripping with all the depth
of derivative low hanging fruit

SICK

It's just a fight and nothing flows
We're all dumbed down and ashamed to glow
We carry scars we never address
We're past caring whether the past's at rest

I don't know how to do this without you
You never show up for me but I always
think you're about to
I'm sick of waiting and sick in general
I want you, not your trifling collateral

It's all pain and no one abides
We're all pulled under and washed out by the tide
We harbor hurt we know not the root of
Our tolerance skyrockets, now we need a new drug

You can't hope to find more meaning
than my heart slick in your hands gleaming
You're sick of stagnation and sick of serenades
You want no one and nothing but your own lonely grave

VOCABULARIES

We're too potent
to be victims
so we'll call it
something else
Every time
we're victimized
our vocabularies
will swell

I'LL HELP YOU FIND IT

My phone autocorrected *don't* to *song*
Gave the impression I find melody
in your unwinding

"All over now," you messaged me
"Gonna do it" (about making yourself bleed)

So I said what you say
Fixed the typo and
messaged back "Don't"
hoping the story wasn't already wrote

Should've said more
Should've been more too
Should've pinged your location
and gone to just be with you

Whether you would have me or not
Even if I'm the only back-up I brought

But I only said "Don't"
then stared at my screen, unblinking
Needing your reply
before I could sleep easy
Instead of just laying there, brain screaming
"You know how he gets
when he can't stop thinking"

"How he needs supernovas of violence
to drown out thought with feeling"

How your self becomes your target
How you hammer boxer breaks into your fists
How that thin blade draws fine red lines
How you say when you're mad
one day you'll graduate to "real" knives

Are you mad enough tonight
How could I let you out of my sight

All this twisting my heart up in my head
'til my blood is rushing in my ears
and I'm all pent-up adrenaline
spiked with sharp tongues
of unrelenting worry
until at long last
you message back, "Sorry"

I'm like, *sorry for what*
For how many injuries this time
inflicted on your own body
and both of our minds

Then you say, "I need help"
and I think, *why, because you went too deep*
Because nightmare mode's the new normal
Because you're still alive but I already grieve

You repeat yourself, "I know I need help"
I manage to text back, "I'll help you find it"
before I collapse back in bed and cry
hoping this is the start
of putting this behind us

ON PURPOSE

Light shining through water, tossing a rainbow

Being led astray, finding new ways home

Kicking rocks, happy a homie kicks back

Hogging the flavor and timing the attack

Making sense, making believe it's on purpose

A legacy I'm coming to terms with

Working the words so they're worth it

DON'T MAKE ME GET MEAN

Breaking loose my secret beast
Disappointing conditional police

I'm scrubbed and, baby, I'm fragranced
but civilization can't even cage this

Just biting my prey
Just making them afraid

Deep in the thicket
Grown up wicked

Wicked animal tensing to chase
Wicked how ravenous I seem to stay

Breaking skin and baring teeth
This meal's mine, don't make me get mean

I'm dressed to the nines, love, and my ensemble fits fine
but if society crowds me, some won't survive

Just prowling around, utterly unleashed
Just tracking a scent that tastes like a treat

Crepuscular in the underbrush
Crouching low, heart in the hunt

Heart finally healing, remembering how
wholeness is my natural state

Heart high on hope precisely evolved for
its ecosystem to sustain

IT'S NOT TOO LATE

Looks like I'll have to do things differently
No more hitting and missing intermittently
Gotta buckle down and not knuckle under
Reclaim my mind and unearth wonder
Howling dogs and circling bats
New dawn awaits and darkness won't last
Yesterday droned on destitute
My meaning got lost and my muse went mute
But there's a part of me that still knows what to do
Power through and write what's true
What's true is I've been stuck here coming unglued
Eyes shut tight conjuring up a better view
than the sorry sight of the aimless life I've led
Letting liars and defilers get in my head
Enough of that and enough of losing
Enough blood bled and enough ego bruising
I'll limp towards love 'til I'm fit to outrun
demons and downfalls with shackles undone
I've got friends I know would hide me
from the consequences I've been inviting
but I can face into the fire
and find the poems burning down inspires
I always knew I wasn't born to wallow
without evolving cocooned in squalor
Without challenging the trauma traders
who corrupt you, crush you, and leave you cratered
So I say here and now I'm in this fight
I'll stop living wrong and fumble towards right
I'll make my mother in Heaven feel proud
I'll show up on time to show what I'm about

It's something I learned but forgot to remember
when every turn I took was another dead ender
When every trick I knew the devil knew too
When tawdry temptation was a damn heady brew
I can't unwaste a single day
but I can pray it's not too late
I can't shoulder sad sick shame
so I'm setting out to redeem my name
I'm here and I'll recognize what's mine
Grab what I'm given tight when stars align
I won't say fuck it, I'll say faster
Speed is my steed for skirting disaster

METTLE

Time is forever running out

Words can never fill it up

Night keeps falling and receding

Hallucinations draw real blood

I can't understand a thing being said

The social fabric is stitched around me

I rip it apart trying to take part

Denying my wounds need suturing

Left alone over and over

Daylight keeps trying to rouse me to action

Each time it dawns I seek some revelation

Sometimes I get one

Sometimes nothing happens

except I realize again how old I've gotten

How much I'm losing whatever the plot is

How many friends I've lost

How many resigned their posts

Gave up that valiant watch or gave up their ghosts

Am I a ghost who just won't give up

A zombie making shambling effort to sprint

I'll recall my mettle momentarily

Sometimes I just need a minute

I FEEL A CHANGE

Finding ways to map
my own terrain
no matter what bars the way
because I feel a change

Drugs just aren't enough
I call that demon's bluff
They're for enhancement
They're not the enchantment
That's the meat of
the argument's thrust

The argument against being a prisoner
making a prize of scant light
The argument in favor of coming back to life

Along my path
plenty of pitfalls
My steady pulse relaxes my roll
I don't have to pick a poison
when I can pick a prism
to pre-emptively refract
a threatening panic attack back
so trepidation doesn't
stab so sharp
So I remember
I'm swift and smart

I can pick my way
through a gauntlet of dangers
Like the abject terror
of loving my neighbors
instead of staying away
Staying strangers
when we're all trying to shake
the things despair named us

THE TRUTH

Saying pretty day is quite a cliché

but I'm going to say it anyway

The truth stays the truth you see

The poem's not wrong 'cos it's easy

Simple to say but means a lot

Like love the world that you got

Like it's not so bad after all

UNTAMED

There's always promise as long as there's music
Melody and treble with wild potential
Crashing untamed through the depths of the den
you retreat into when you're feeling animal

To keep your peace, tuck under your wings
Hide from any eyes by averting your own
Taking some time to be at home being alone

There's always power as long as there's lyrics
or instruments singing with pre-verbal meaning
You get it somehow, somewhere deep down
It's sound that saves
salvos a message for each listener individually and
imparts core truth to everyone intrinsically

You realize you've always been missing
this particular storm of sonics
Until musicians sense them and go after them
songs are long lost spirits

Dropping under surfaces, dropping into trance
Bearing witness to a network of myriad longings
Taking rapture's hand to dance

I'll never be unmoved by the scathing soul of rock and roll
Never be too deaf to slow my stroll and appreciate hip hop's flow
Never presume to interrupt the enlivening blast of riotous guitar
Never fail to get goosebumps when a frontman nails a snarl

It's connection to the other realms
It's celebration of the divine, irrepressible spark
It's art that helps you fight to survive
Gives you anthems to sing in the dark
Anthems swelling and sliding sumptuously
Anthems to spite the dull, desensitizing drag
Anthems so strong the same song can evolve
to mean new and different things, adeptly filling different needs
Recognizing silent screams we could never quite unleash
Music lets us out of captivity
Disassembles and rebuilds us endlessly
I'm not who I was before I encountered my favorite songs
Crank up the eclectic stylings and savor the sound of raising ceilings
at the same time as you blow out the walls

Every time I hit repeat on certain songs
I come home to some other sublime stratosphere
It reaches me at the deep-down depths
It hones me just to hear

Refine my chorus, sift a love song for us
Dare me to show my dedication, to tribute your maniac radiance
Your chrysalis crescendo
Your big, bad, buck wild bridge
Your winsome, worthy words
Your croon smooth and slick

Oh inward gazing epic finale, oh operatic hurricane
The songs you know by heart are the songs that know your name
Have always had your number,
Felt you in that first interaction and had you sized
as irreverent interloper impossibly intrepid
inviting music's meaning inside to bed down in harmonious mind

It's all getting so orchestral, now it's morphing into metal
Now it's blending to power ballad
Now melody balms your madness malady
The righteous tide has to roll back out eventually

No, don't accept it, play it again, play it back, play it backwards
to bring out a B-side transmission
Song's story is sprawling and expansive
The arrangements compact and tight,
Music to make you wanna slowly sway
Music to fill you up with fight

It accepts us in, we're lucky
It caresses us, we're loved
It blares off our blindfolds, we're dazed, amazed and drugged

and no, it never has to end
and maybe it never will
Some of us it lifts to move, some of us get still
Not wanting to miss a nourishing note
Not wanting to leave any innovation unsavored
Soundtracking our loves and losses and labors

Coming on like a mad god drummer
Mad to know us, mad *because* of knowing us,
Giving us gifts of sleeper sneakers and crossover smash hits
Both ever unfolding under
umbrellas of genres that splice and twist

Oh these dulcet deviations, oh this suite of halcyon
Even if everything thinks it's over, song will birth itself anew
to rock the next world's dawn

HIVE MIND

Did you get your way
from the universe
after all this time
Pried from jealousy's maw
while it glared with
seething green eyes

How it can hurt so
waiting your turn
Acting unconcerned while
solitude burns

Did you finally corner your
coveted company
without the hive mind
crowding you out
Hissing, "Do you really think
you can reach anyone
unless we say it's allowed?"

I pray the weight of your winnings
will finally be enough
I hope you got yours and
got away unengulfed

CELEBRATE YOU

I love you although
like always I'm late

I didn't want to be high when you
saw me for the last time

So I waited to sober up
Meanwhile you died

I'm sorry for that
I'll always be sorry

There was no funeral
I missed the remembrance ceremony

Unable to listen to the lectures
and weather the "there he is" looks

From people who weren't there
for our history of hurt

The times you clawed my face all up
with your pretty press-on nails

The night you wouldn't let me stay
So my dogs and I slept with our backs to hay bails

The times it was you who wasn't there
The times when you were there but weren't really you

The hazardous times when your embittered addiction
was sure to cut me down if I spoke or moved

None of which is an excuse for my inaction
but my reason is I just couldn't deal

I knew you were slipping away and I thought
turning my back on it meant it wouldn't be real

I talk to you and I believe
you're still here in a way

I forgive you without reservation
I mean it when I say

It's not enough
I'm a bad son

Like you always said
I've always been

But I hope even a bad seed
can still be forgiven

Because I get now how some substance can
scoop you out of yourself and let a monster take over

I've raged as long and loud as you used to
Violent and convinced of my victimhood

I know you couldn't control it
Do you know there are things I can't control

Like the nightmares where you chip away at me still
for not doing like I'm told

Like the days I can barely move
because I still expect to be punished for moving

Days my existence seems like something
I'm inflicting on the world

When anyone professing to love me
leaves me wallowing in confusion

Yet I forgive you anyway
No matter what the scars say

I hope you forgive me too
No matter what I didn't do

No matter where I wasn't
What you wanted me to be that I couldn't

I'm not angry except in the yesterdays
When we commune I celebrate you

ALIVE

Here I go again, just can't stop

You say hope's gone, I think not

Scuffed up but alive and still kicking

Gonna blow up soon, hear the ticking

It'll paint the world such lovely colors

Spirits will lift, we'll embrace one another

Believe in that day, it's a stunner

ULTRA UNDERGROUND

I really don't know what'll come out next
or how it'll make the subtext text
I genuinely don't and I wish I did
We can find out together
Buckle up kid

My leg won't stop shaking
Feel like I'm tap dancing on a tightrope
More like a livewire
Pretending there's vitamins in the volts

I don't want to unsheathe an edge
Don't want to soften corners
Don't want no heavy filters
approved by no gatekeeping consortium

Maybe it's not about their definition
or their misdefinition
Maybe it's all about what
it can all mean to us

Maybe it's so ultra underground
it doesn't catch a buzz

But then maybe I'm reaching
stellar souls one by one
here and there

My people
Resistant
Vigilant
Artful and aware

RESURRECT

It's a lie when dark damns
the total summed
from the whole soul of a man
Do you think it's always
night in your mind
Can you resurrect
the remains of a good day

One that got you blinkered
for some brolic badass besotted
He told you, "Tuck your tongue in, buddy,
I need to be spotted"
and you said, "Lift me, lunkhead,
if 160 pounds isn't a problem"
So he stood you on a broom handle
and bench-pressed you to build his body
and you got a good look at
his vascular virtues
and entered deeper into
his easy camaraderie

That's a memory to crystalize
when slavering shadows materialize
Your mind can free you from the misery
You've just got to realize
you're stronger than the stranglehold
when sadness is a riptide

Just give yourself credit
where credit's due
There are untold depths
of strength in you

In the morning tell
the truth to the dawn
if last night's dreams
are a bad trip you're still on
Sorrow's shape and
nebulous nothingness
headlock your inner vision
but if you focus your synaptic fire
you can vaporize the figments

Can you resurrect
your barely buried brilliance
blindingly beautiful on the day
you broke bread with
the best friends you could ask for
and one of them said
"I couldn't withstand it
if I loved you any more"
and you said
"I'm glad I've got you
It means I've got all the luck"
and you shared each other's food
and lifted each other up

That's a memory to center
on the days that are dementors
Your heart can help you through the horror
You've only got to enter
your own power's inner chamber
to conquer what torments you

Just give yourself grace
where grace is deserved
You got all the guts you need
and plenty of nerve

MAYBE THIS TIME

The nightmares got so bad I gotta take medicine to stop them.

The southern night makes so many sounds, its music rejuvenates my vibration.

The seizure seized me and then let me go, leaving me jittery and jarred deep down.

The thing is, other life must be out there somewhere, maybe it don't wanna be found.

The hairline's patchy, the gut protruding, in pictures I see how I've aged.

The truth is, it's down to us to save each other, or else we don't deserve to be saved.

The form might not be fit anymore, a thing it shakes me some to admit.

The fact remains, if there's a war for your soul to be fought, mine requires I fight in it.

The fatigue lasts forever, I seem to have energy to burn only when tossing in bed.

The birds and bugs sing a duet so solid, listening soothes my Restless Leg.

The stress shows up as neck pain, throbbing as random and splintered as lightning.

The bad dreams have always been with me, but maybe this time they won't find me.

FINEST KIND

The best first impressions will eventually be tarnished. Stick around, I tell myself, not every era can be golden. It's no one person's fault. Tension flares because it's flammable. Even loving hearts sometimes get afflicted by hateful sentiments going viral.

I don't know why we can't always overflow with generosity. Why we can't always remember to judge each other charitably. Why the benefit of the doubt is dismantled by familiarity, even though it confirms our skill at recognizing character to stick with our initial instincts.

But don't stay cruel and ugly, because I hate labeling you thusly. Because I can see in the lines of your face that it drains your strength, which I know to be considerable. I've seen your quiet resolve deepen in kindness and power to offset another's sadistic meanness. You catching the bug yourself is the only thing I've yet seen that has made your voice falter, or your feet stumble for even a step.

I don't know why exactly you're not yourself right now. But I know it would carve you up to be reminded of it later. I have faith you're gonna snap back and I won't rub your face in any of this shit when that happens. Maybe the real you — so solid, so decent and resilient — was too seriously taken advantage of. Maybe you haven't seen enough signs of karma doing its job, or you were an innocent bystander caught in the crossfire when someone sicker ducked out of the way of karma's big gun. Whatever it is, I'm here to help you through it. I'm here to help, so I'll try and absorb it. Because this is the first time you've ever presented me any characteristic it felt wrong to honor.

Remember when you told me you'd stay with me 'til I got the results of that scary test? Remember when you came to my rescue when my car died on the road and I got showered in downed power lines and cascading shatterglass? I do, and I remember all the moments since, where I tried to find the words or actions to be there for you the way the finest kind of friend surely deserves. This is me still doing that, because I know that man is still who you are.

You're no catty gossip. You're not a vindictive blinded blinder. You're not at all any of what you're manifesting now. I'm resolute God wants me to refuse to believe any of this. To refuse to think ill of you unless and until this performance shows itself as a pattern of behavior. Not just a one-off anomaly, out of step with the rhythms of your goodness.

One day, maybe, I'll need you to do the same for me. To deny my worst reactions to whatever small imperfections on anyone's part add up to bamboo slid under my nails. If so, I trust you not even to remind me of it, the way I won't remind you of this episode, which I'm keeping no record of. There will be no entry about you for today's date in my heart or brain's memory banks.

I know that. I know I'll forget this. I'm certain it's forgettable, because anyone has the right to disappoint anyone, but I also have the right not to be disappointed. Instead, I'll look forward to my high hopes being vindicated. This is a scene too insignificant to include in your biography. It just muddies waters needlessly. It doesn't track with the thrust of your inspiring true story.

THROTTLE

Run it down and throttle it
just to prove who's badder
What an unfortunate soft animal
drifting in range of your temper
I hope we both escape you
I'm just gonna be honest
I hope you snatch
at my sleeve when I leave
and catch only a little stardust

HOPE ANYWAY

I hear you say you'll never let anyone in
I'm anyone, so I'm not on the list
I know you keep yourself roped off
and that you won't admit it if I turn you on

It seems chances are thinner
with each passing day
I understand all of this
and hope anyway

I see you pack up your room and move
I'm left behind, imagining you
I guess you've gotten good at running
and my busted heart's barely fit for walking

It looks like betting on you
costs more than I can pay
I've done the math
and hope anyway

I find you on Facebook, posting pretension
Comes off just right, as mean as you intended
I try to think you'll be kinder when you
remember to miss me
and swear by my senses you won't
so easily dismiss me

It feels like you're on some distant moon
I sure wasn't built to wait
When you return I doubt you'll stay
and hope anyway

You come back to town, duded out in fresh duds
You bring the down, I bring the up
We enjoy each other and that gets you mad
but I'm not about to apologize for that

I got you figured out as best I can
As much as anyone ever could
I know it's no game and you don't play
but I try to have fun and hope anyway

AS I PLEASE

To calm back down, own my errors

Sleep as I please, defying night terrors

Root well, spared stabs of shallow spades

Race with grace until flicker and fade

Never again open the jugular of hope

Fatten those famine left just hollow bones

Be me the jubilee, alive, not alone

IMPOSSIBLE MUSIC

Cooling drizzle calms me down
'til I'm not worried, my nerves stop jangling
I can settle into a siesta
It can just happen naturally

Meditation still eludes me at first
because of a rising tide
of impossible music
A barely decipherable discordant squall
Guitars gone catastrophic
Melody mutated, guttural
It doesn't quite center me but
I don't let it trouble

I fall short of remote viewing but
I find my mind reaching out and fine tuning
this soundtrack from death metal's
twisted mirror dimension
It harmonizes with my hum
My vibe finds its beat again

Hammock bound, counting clouds
streaked through with shocks of gray
Gray punched through with dancing rays

All of me exhales at last
I allow my superego to catch up to me
Soothe it with assurances
that I agree with it about everything

Just give me time, I request of the me
that makes his appearance when
I'm cranked to chill
Time to break in good influence's fit
so my shadow doesn't chafe
I gotta show it that it's safe
It doesn't always need to stay awake

For now I just wanna drift a little
Restored by the gift of good weather
Breathing deep the fresh air
while it still blesses the lucky biosphere
Mining a lullaby from the raw ore of racket
Inexplicably getting away with relaxing

PRIMAL POWERS

There's no limit to the infinite
or to the subatomic
You can always go bigger
Always go smaller
That's how it works in God's arithmetic

Sometimes it feels like you can't stand it
The forces pulling you outward and apart
The forces driving you to shrink within
but you are made of primal powers
just like everything

Think of how strong you've already been
How often you've been reconfigured and lived
The times you found even more to give
though you felt entirely depleted

The pebble in the ocean gets
sanded down but persists
Its basic building blocks remain
even when microscopic

The asteroid belt in the
reaches of space scatters far
but there's plenty of room to
sprawl out among stars

Plenty of room to buckle and reshape among friends
I promise the breakdown isn't the end

There isn't an end
There is only transformation
Remember that always
when you're feeling impatient

BRING THE HEAT

Still there's strut in my step
no matter what all is wrong with me
Got a lead foot on the pedals
and when feet beat streets
That's how I bring the heat
Look at me now
with meaning replete

ESCAPE ROUTE

The land we live on borders the national park
We get the bobcats, the odd black bear
We get owls and foxes and possums
and scores upon scores of deer

They're all beautiful, the views are all scenic
I appreciate the grandeur but I'm not happy here
I'm not fully formatted for the country
even after all this time
I want options; I need to oscillate

The stillness soothes but sometimes enervates
I'm so tired of getting my rest
So bored of my own company
but not as bored as I am of trolling the local rednecks

It's still a half-a-horse town
but at least now we have a new farmer's market
A proud newfangled pavilion
I pretend it's exciting so I don't feel heartless

Everyone's been talking about it
Saying it's a project thirty years in the making
Like farmers here cater to some underserved niche
Like produce is inherently life-changing

Perhaps I'm cynical about their noble profession
It's just that I'd rather they build a gay bar
or at least fix up and re-open the theater
Both would provide some passing means of escaping
That's how I know we'll never get either

My mind doesn't always feel like camping
I love nature but I also crave culture
Most all I get here is the chance to bone up on bird hierarchies
How murders govern their members
The order of succession in a committee of vultures

Circling circling circling
The drain the drain the drain
Wrath pours from the clouds
The power goes out
What fun, we're really roughing it now

Someone send a helicopter
Someone fire a flare
If only I wasn't talking to myself
If only some sugar daddy would hear

I'm too old to keep on aging here
I want to gray established in a city
Compassion for other men is too cosmopolitan
to be a value of your typical hillbilly

It's not manly to have an emotional life
To feel some type of way about becoming frail and elderly
ensconced in isolation; given frights by heteronormativity
Falling down or having trouble getting around, like feeling,
is an embarrassing vulnerability

Maybe my verses will make their way out
Maybe in that way connection to
the core of my calling might survive
This is my flare, my heroic helicopter
This is my escape route I write

BATTLE

Stare down cesspools
Skinny as a scarecrow

Skip past skinheads
On the inside wearing rainbow

Lie to looky-loos leaning in
about how far out you've been

Reject the premise of the game
Sometimes not playing is how you win

Spend the cheddar
on feeding the neighborhood

Reconstitute solidarity
Show up where you said you would

Speak truth to power
resisting the impulse to duck and cover

Cleave to ultimate truism
Battle battle, be not just bluster

SOMEPLACE

It's another day I'm lucky to be alive
even without much sun and
the sky concrete gray

I put my shoes and jacket on
Then my smile
Telling myself it'll take me someplace

Middle-aged growing pains
and imbibed numbing agents
proved ineffective against
distant hope's radiance

My hands look empty but they're not
Only dimly aware of the strength they've got

I could've died so many times
but since I'm living I'll try
to be worthy of this life

I know my mistakes and misdeeds surround me
Carnivores that dart in and tear away chunks
False friends who come calling out of memory
Calling in favors they croon for
with the silkiest tongues

I turn them away
Put them aside
I gave in before and some light in me died

I believe in possibility
That it'll wink back on
before steadily beaming
by the next dreamy dawn

I lackadaise down the gravel lane
without betraying to the world
my heightened hurry
No particular destination yet
but today that won't deter the journey

Worry preoccupies but this body
is moved by my own mind
It lives to make its own luck
Determined to thrive

WHAT ALL I LIKE

I like this journal
The pages are heavy
I'm getting after it
Attacking it with poetry

I like dogs whose paws
run on air in their sleep
and cats who do the
flirt flop in front of you

I'm reacquainting myself
with what all I like
'cos I remembered joy
belongs to me too

I like the way you lean
when you say "Yo"
Tilting forward like you
might fall on me

I'd like the chance to catch you
in my arms like in my dreams

I like blue blue blue blue blue
in all variations
Splashed all over everything

I'm tripping out of tune
but I also like to sing

I like food food food food food
Savored and shared
or mine all mine voraciously

I like a man whose appetites
easily outmatch his apathy

Comics from Marvel I really like
I like writing poems about Gambit

If you're injured or falling ill
I like riding with you
in the ambulance

I like a lot of things I recall
This list could get quite long
but mostly I like it when you're here
more than when you're gone

VITAL VIBE

A fruit-shaped candy as an icebreaker, an open heart, a promise in the making, a gift of tied-up, bright felt flowers, a general store, a half-dozen for a dollar, a day of gold, eyes sky blue, time divided into "Before You" and "After You," an original film cell from a Marvel movie, a deep, long kiss to tell you I love it, a crumpled mess made of it after an hours-long argument, an angry wound on a swollen knee, you needing help and looking at me, me needing help with a bone-level throbbing, your sketchpads, my notebooks, our jawing and jotting, a night of cooling humors, arrogant tempers, the hottest, most humid season on record, an asset unalloyed, taken in the spirit of gift giving, wordplay at cross-purposes, reckless proclivities encouraged, an obvious impossibility, a mind that flatly rejects it, a symphony, a sugaring, a cross-pollination, a run-through of a monologue about why we're destined always to drift apart, a rebuttal of the whole premise, bigger plans than ever for the muse you still are, a calendar flipping fast, another year of vacillating, gone quicker than a daydream in the clamor of dishes shattering, breakfast in bed, seasoned with glass shards and floored, a broom and dustpan, mop and bucket, hope a dirigible unmoored, a fevered fight, a washcloth rung, your sweat rolling through the lines on the palms of my hands, proof we're still connecting, a qualified agreement, a gathering up of each other, sharing a bit of breathwork, clutching a bit of zen, you siding with me against spiritual sabotage, a peace offering of acknowledgment, a stare right past me, perched on your sickbed, cropped from a picture you're already amending, an eleventh hour optimism, a pretense too far for fetching, beer bottles clinking, that long ago summer, a toast to imbroglio and excess, a vital vibe we knew we had, never knowing how long it would last, offering up love without agreeing on how much, a spirit splinted, your graceful, slender back, my guts all akimbo watching you go, as you sprint to a cab, a ripping down the middle, a sectioning, a me staying behind without you, a me breaking ranks to keep you in view, a lot to say, more to cut, a thousand gossipy, wagging tongues, a construction-paper valentine like they pass out in grade school, a racy, scribbled salutation on it from someone new who's a version of you, a time to move on, a troubled past to unbind, a truth told to taunt, a well-timed, harmless lie, another chance I refuse to miss out on right after it's gone, a scheme I dare not dream, a road lit bright by starlight, a full head of steam, an innocence amputated from sordid, sinful lives, me still pedestaling you, you admitting you don't hope I die, what joyful generosity, this meeting each other where we live, a show seasoned, shut down, revivaling, the best it's ever been

SIMPATICO

I'm rambling
I'm reveling
I'm bedeviling
I'm flexing my
entire fragged brain

Fatalistic, tawdry triptych
Some vignettes are best beheld
in soft focus
Baby bandied about
Brutalized
'til they bastardized belief

At an impasse abandoned
with a brand new essential tremble
The quietest livewire
Resigned to keeping
any tenuous peace

When we two war
it's a hell of a thing
Hatchets unburied
Real heft behind their swings

But somehow
Only sometimes
Like this time
We've surprised each other
sampling sounds
of more simpatico songs

Sharing a cordial word
A common rhythm
Catching each other noticing
An awkward eagerness
we don't comment on

Still, cadence says a lot without lyrics
Says it all in stereo
that pretty soon we'll be keeping
time and tempo
with most every moment of
one another's music

It's new to us, this status
as neighborly non-combatants
Easing into alliance
Deepening into dalliance
that quickens 'til we're
barely calm enough
to use the last of our control
to agree on just how to lose it

A negotiation abbreviated
A work of art undressed
Our symphony hot and heavy metal
Rolled by waves that crest and crest

A GLIMPSE

A glimpse of your face
The sum of sideways glances
could make anybody wonder
if maybe you could love them

I've looked you full in the face
There is no sum for that
Just trust me when I tell you
I'm wondering a lot

I've looked beyond your face
where nothing's by the numbers
Where formulae break down
and silver tongues aren't worth much

I don't have a silver tongue, by the way
I just practice praising you every morning
in case I accidentally run into you
By the way, it's never an accident

FAVORITE VILLAIN

Oh no, big baller
your disarming smile only
begs these backwoods boys for harm

They skin you 'cross the court
then laugh as they take their ball
and head home

Leave you tending
a diversity of wounds
Cursing your senses for not
side-stepping sharp elbows
For getting close enough
to make an impact
The arm hooked around your throat
didn't rob you of that

What now, evildoers,
turning back to glare at you
like someone just told them
what "pillage" means
and they wanna prove you
still got some things to lose

Why must they hurt
Is it the only way they know to touch
Do you think it enrages one among them
to secretly need it so much

All the abrasions dished out by your favorite villain
His eyes closed softly like it's just how he kisses
Such an innocent face, just mind where his fist is

Get back, devil dissemblers,
Finally there are Samaritans joining your side
You've got witnesses, got your wits about you

In the face of this fact, they flee
fifty strides before they realize no one's chasing

You're busy, you got some love now, and
you've always had lyricism

You let the bad guys get away
as if that'll save them
Too target locked to change where they're aiming

Let him try to find an excuse now
to show up when he can't stay away

When touch is no longer enough
He will need one blessed taste
Don't give it unless he's brave

CONSTANT DAYDREAM

I must have been daydreaming
about the impossibility
I'm determined to achieve

You must have been
just waiting
to douse it with the bracing
water of reality

It's a beautiful day anyway
The kind the sun and the breeze
equally kiss your face
A good day to be in love
Even if I'm the only one

You don't seem happy
or better without me
You wouldn't want it
to be over
once it begun
Have you even considered
the idea of us

I'd romance your reticence
'til it was displaced by certitude
and prologue could finally
give way to interlude

I'd stay with you
or follow you
Come find you
if you lose yourself
Any peril or problem
I'd find a way to help

Why do I maintain
this pursuit
as punishing so far
as it is unrewarding
It's like you got
my most shining aspirations
tied down for waterboarding

Most involve making you mine
Making us ours
This constant daydream
will come true
Damn our crossed stars

HALFWAY

After all this time
will you finally meet me
Halfway to learning
who I am?
If you do, we can be confident
Neither of us will forget
either of us again

BEYOND OUR MEANS

What about running away together
for an hour or weekend or
fortnight or forever

Following some creek
Collecting smooth stones
for skipping while we're skipping
paying what we owe

It accrued so quickly
Interest when we weren't looking
All we wanted was a one-bedroom
for eating, sleeping and smoking
Fucking around and fucking off
Being together even at odds
Helpless about how hard we're hoping

Well not much scares me anymore
now that a one-bedroom
proved beyond our means
Bankrupt for the time being

Time just
being
Just laying there or
flopping bonelessly

Let's trace some ley lines
Steal some succulence
Sneak our way into
some party of opulence

Make like Remy Lebeau
Liberate artifacts and high-end trinkets
I know we can do it because I can think it

I know we can fence it if we can free it
If we wear it for all they know we could be it

DIVE DEEP

Scooch on over
Reach out
Beckon me in
Make an effort
and find it twinned
By me newly emboldened
I just look at you
and I gotta leap
I'm not after what comes cheap
so wade in and dive deep
I feel so adrift
when we part company
Embrace me again
Don't make it perfunctory
Don't just run out the clock
before you send me shambling home
Size up my heart
C'mon, claim what you own
Open up to me further
Shut down my inhibition
and my love won't fail you
Loving you well is my mission
It's why I was sent here
at the same time as you
I give you my word
that every word's true
when I say you're the landmark
I find my bearings with
It's no good as a map
if your position's not on it

You're the heart I head for
The lyric most apt
Singing me out of my doldrums
Coaxing me out of safe shadows
Desire seems dangerous
but living without you is more so
You're my true north
My weakness
My afterglow
My strength for the lengths
to which I'd gladly go
To amaze you
To exhilarate you
'cos hot damn you're my jam
All I want is all of you
All yours is all I am

HAPPIEST

Despite everything, you remain
fundamentally kind
That's why I'm letting you know
I'm proud of you
That you're a hero in my eyes

It makes me so damn angry
what your poisonous abuser put you through
if you got a bead on his current location
I'll fuck him up for you

I hope you know now that nothing can stop you
from bouncing back, or remembering how to laugh
I hope you know you're easy to care about
My heart was kind of keeping that a secret
but consider me caught in the act

I like you in your garden
where you go both to escape and to feel present
Standing beside you the other day
while you told me what grows where
The breeze on my skin, the sun on my face
felt like we crossed the border into Heaven

This isn't my best ever deciphered translation
Unless by "best ever" you mean "most true"
It's only clumsily poetic, like an amateur said it
But I'm a little nervous this time
'Cos this time, it's for you

We oughta catch a movie sometime
We oughta catch lightning bugs
You oughta catch me falling
You oughta try my touch

You're a flurry of productive movement most times
Always exiting and re-entering the room
Always finding worthy projects
Creating things to do
And that's fine; that's great; it's to be commended
You're not the type to just sit on your ass
but I've been trying to find a moment
to make an impression on you
and do it with some measure of class

It's not me to just grab you without consent
I guess I'm more the kind to 'fess up in a simple poem
That my agenda is centered on seeing you smile
That you're the person I'm happiest to know

THE ULTIMATE EPIC

I dream that at last
you fall and fall hard
We get fiery without
risking our friendship

It's just like it is
in the movies
but better
because when it's not
just a story
there's no necessity
of conflict

Which doesn't mean
there aren't stories
Even in the
everyday minutiae
we find epic impetus

We become the
ultimate epic
about sustainable peace

You let me tell you
how you gave that to me
in moments never over
now that they're logged
in my memory of feeling

Like when you told me
the demonic voice
that drags me
is a liar
and you scooted
a little closer
and it made
a big difference

Just being awash
in what you radiate
making up for
the pain of existence

WELL OF WANTING

I reach, I tear the hours apart in flames
My heart a furnace burning through the sky
as hunger roots within my soul in chains
and echoes of your voice refuse to die

I hear the moonstone cries within the deep
where shadows kiss the skin of days that run
and through the cavern's veil, I cannot sleep
The well of wanting pulls me to the sun

Oh might I touch the restless waves of air
and pull your name from every star's embrace
To lose myself where none but you is there
and drown in longing's cruel and burning grace

For every breath is empty 'til I find
the world that lives inside your grasping mind

HIS COURAGE

Today, as my fate would have it

I met a mystic fueled by passion

Calm in his courage, made of magic

One moment gentle, the next one savage

How close I came to giving up

Before he arrived, all easy to love

What I wished for, we have become

NEWS OF FIRES

Waiting on replies, reading news of fires
sweeping the region
Is it safe to sleep again

Can't make many shapes out
in such wispy clouds
Can't smell past the smoke of the
whole town burning down

Soon the sky will be gray
and clogged with ash
We can call it an effigy and
eulogize the past

The times I grabbed your hands
and I could feel that you felt it
No matter what nerves
were damaged or deadened

The nights we did nothing and that was fine
The nights one of was sure but
the other couldn't decide

Your technicolor flamboyance
busted knuckles
rendered rugged

My taciturn frustration
when you were most indifferent
and most beloved

The night coming alive around us
with bats and owls
and lightning bugs

You stumbling
stammering drunk
the first time we ever hugged

Now I'm just waiting on replies
while perusing
a roster of guys

Expecting nothing from you
except love gone to waste
and thoughts that race

Not looking for someone
who struts like you
but another flavor profile
A distinct, different taste

A brand-new kind of true blue
to join me here
disbelieving the view

Feel the heat bake the air and
see flames encroaching
Safe as houses anyway
Both of us just knowing

HEARD YOU TELL IT

I'm kicking and you're screaming
You're giving ground and I'm digging in
We are not who we've been

You're a gaslight and I'm a brushfire
I'm a crank and you're the dank
We both keep expecting a shank

And if I heard you tell it
You'd say I was lucky you found me
And if you heard me tell it
I'd say your arrogance astounds me
and pounds me and drowns me
like a wave I start to crave

I feel wired and you feel mired
You're all about the old school and all I know
is I'm not flunking
We're both alarming aggression junkies

You're an edgelord and I'm an empath
I'm on edge and you're on point
Our handling of each other is getting adroit

And if you heard me tell it
I'd say I know I opened myself up to this
And if I heard you tell it
You'd say you guess I got my wish
and too much is still
not enough of this

I'm tipsy and you're testy

Your skin thickens and my heart bleeds
but each of us on the other feeds

You're a good teacher and I'm a quick study
I'm your favorite hobby and you're my passion project
There's a gravity between us
we best learn to respect

And if I heard you tell it
You'd say this whole thing is inconvenient
And if you heard me tell it
I'd say damn right but I know
you're feeling it
and the next storm between us
batters skies 'til they split
but choppy waters right this ship

PERCENTAGES

Once again writing is all
that might save me
Even when my thoughts
are too diffuse
to know exactly what I'm saying

Like if I said I hate loving you
would I want you to believe it

If this ends between us
won't all of me grieve it

Will I instantly implode
or will it punch holes in my heart
to end me by pinpricks
Will you ever even know
a shade of the emptiness
you leave me with

You're decimating me right now
with your dismissive batting down
of my every salient
point or concern

With convenient canned rejoinders
All my fault, yes, I know
Yes, I know, *I never learn*

Once again ink
might as well be blood
Need feels like death
Even when I get what I want
it's quick to bed
then easily fled

If you said you'd stay with me
would you wish you hadn't
Would my fried attention span
even be able to handle it

Would all of you
end up leaving me
or would you leave me
with your echo
Would I ever even know
if it came from
outside or inward

I'm decimating you right now
so I never need find out
Telling truths that break
your good heart by percentages

Just know it's not your fault
It's my need for endlessness that ended this

SWEAR

I will get in your heart's good humor
I swear by my grit and my wit
I will find every secret to your fun

THE SUM OF US

Laughed off, that's how I feel
After we laughed together for so many years
Pulling together to push each other's buttons
Cruising night streets in the country
under too many stars to wish on

You were the home I wanted, each and every one
You never had to stay young or innocent
to remain my inspiration

What happened to us
We were a crew that kept it lively
Everywhere we went, we kept each other from dying
How I wish those days were now
though the closet still kept me then
and my secret seemed so deadly
I was always dialing myself down

I'm persevering on my own
but I remember our ardent oath
How we'd never lose each other
to the next bend in the road

I remember our psyches entwining
I remember paper and sugar cubes on our tongues
I don't remember agreeing on
a certain age to give each other up

We used to share cigarettes and blunts
We used to share our fears, unafraid
Harbored hope so bioluminescent
    it always lit our way
no matter the darkness that came

I can't feel my way through shadow
    to any of you now
You who never left love unspoken
   when you knew I needed
   such things spelled out

What will become of me now
  if I'm the last to disavow
  I thought we'd rendezvous
  at road side sometimes
  but now I've got my doubts

Wherever you made your new world
Dammit, I'm still on this planet with you
  It's been weeks without reply
since I messaged that I still miss you

It doesn't quite add up
  to anything anymore
We drink and smoke in isolation
We hide ourselves from each other like shame
but it's the sum of us we're drowning
  It's never just our pain

It's the sum of us subtracted
Let's add each other again

CERTAIN SKULLDUGGERY

Can't sit still or mind my manners
Ain't rolling out red carpets
About time we dispensed with artifice

You think transcendent thoughts
but some frailties can't be fought
Hopeless to hide when anyone
can follow the blood
Soldier, don't try to stand
Your Achilles is cut

I gave it my best
so you gave it your all
These are days to amaze
Not to dream small
The drab routine
dragged down to drown
What you always meant to mean
is paramount now

Can't sit still or bite my tongue
while petty deceits strike our destinies dumb
You claim you know how to get us
to where we're golden
Well darling don't dismay if
my doubt is emboldened

Your sincerity shines
with every crazy commitment
you swear this time you'll keep
What kills is you could
if you'd admit you're deep

Fair weather friends
fallen in love with fuckery
Sticking with them ensures certain skullduggery
In recompense they trifle with truth
Manifest just enough virtue
to confess villainous voodoo

You gave it your all
so I'll give you my sword
A little swish in my swashbuckle
Still warrior born
When it comes to upholding
your honor adored
I'll cut motherfuckers
be they a handful or a horde

WONDERSTRUCK

I remember how your eyes
were a source of light
How your touch was a current
How your bravery inspired mine

You made me see
a million poems in my mind
overlapping in jubilant flight

The dark kissed your silhouette
You loaned the night your shine

You loaned me your full attention
I mostly used it at first to stare
The depth and breadth of all you meant
left me wonderstruck and slightly scared

Never before had a new arrival
in my life become so essential so soon
For mere minutes well met and yet
I already recognized you

It felt wrong to hold our peace separately
It had to be you and I together
So I trusted you to understand
my feverish endeavor

To connect with the indispensable moment
To find any pretext to touch you
With how rapt I was rendered
How easily
How could I not ache to
What else could I do

You didn't shy away
I didn't shrink from the challenge
For once I didn't feel like
the last lonely soul
fate abandoned

Your arms so strong pulling me close
Your lips eucalyptus
My hand stroking your throat

Did we have an audience
Was anyone else present
I can't remember
It didn't seem important

How did we get there
Did the spectrum of sensation
exist prior to that moment

Did my hands have purpose
before you decided to hold them

Questions still unanswered
Still amazing me to this day
With you still nearby me
minor details escape

STARRY EYES

I know you, north star, needing guidance
Pressured to mark every turn of the map
Cardinal directions always needing you to find them

I eyeball you and pray for cosmic alignment
We found each other, can we find our defiance
I was once a prodigal, and at peace with that
You were once a man possessed
Once we were men emancipated
No force could reckon with

Such bright light, burns out blight
Pierces fog, cuts through lies
Such sacrifice, sweet starry eyes
Incinerating every night
Incendiary love for every
traveler you find

Starry eyes, such delight
to meet you here moonstruck
My guy, the weather's fine
no matter how strong the stormfront
Oh starry eyes, if any force freezes time
I maintain your gravity might
Just try, starry eyes, we let so much slip by
Pull me in, starry eyes, where dimensions divide
Let me make every version of all of you mine
Get you on lock in every timeline

CRACKED OPEN

I see you got your color up
Got them quack-quackers all aligned
That's good; best to be prepared
Too fit to flee, tightened and ripe
for pluck-plucking, berry by berry,
straight from the vine
Any drawbridge will drop for you
Any password you give will do just fine
Go on, go on in
Get everything you can
Wrassle it if you want it
Seize the rays with both hands
The light is all yours, love
No blockheads can block it
Your mind's money-money
No losses to offset

No stinging rebuke
from the sad suckers bamboozled
by your bright brain ballooning
Hopped up on helium
so you can lift what they're losing
You got the funds funneled
into your jingle-jangling pockets
Plink-plink go the goods
from all wishing wells
WABOOSH! says your wallet
Stuffed beyond capacity
Green to match the vista's budding blooms
Vaping casually in the verdant fronds
Backwards ball cap tastefully askew

You're clean as a whistle
Your timbre clear as a bell
You ring-ring-a-ling
for hors d'oeurves from the help
You're the tingle in every taste bud
You make folks just melt
Your hand wins again
Your public wants impaled
You keep a locked lid
on any chef's secret
about how you mix your potent marinade
Sizzle-sizzle goes the tenderized
carefully seasoned mindscape
of the latest hick on your hook, wriggle-wriggling
Stewing in his juices
Senses gone swimmy
Now you're all he sees
Savory and shimmering

Do you know you got a world here
quivering to be cracked open
Do you maintain that detached veneer
to toy with your supplicants' emotions
You've just gotta give us a peek inside
where you keep the real bling-bling
and the freshest freaky style
You could show us how you know us
by the currency we carry
but you just hang loose
and break our blues
busting moves so smooth it's scary

SUMMONERS

Maybe today I'll show you that poem
The better of the two I wrote for you
You can react however feels natural
I'll withstand telling the truth
Maybe what's yours and mine will entwine
Maybe you'll distance and get quiet

There's a volume to someone's quiet
Silence was perhaps the original poem
Your soundlessness and mine might entwine
A buoyant heart is my gift from you
A music felt lifting us like our own shared truth
Thinking you affect me this way on purpose is natural

The supernatural I bet you make natural
Finding each other for lifetimes by the signature of our quiet
Incantations rendered from our instinctive truth
Passed as thoughtforms between us summoners of poem
You co-write me and I co-write you
Choosing our disciplines as enchantments entwine

Our favorite verb should ever remain entwine
Our lurid ideations remain pristine and natural
Always willing to get muddied up for and by you
Soak in your sound heart and share soothing quiet
Every day all about bringing to light the latest poem
Never finished elucidating this central core truth

One serious funny thing about the truth
It spits out any lie that tries to entwine
Even if the lies might make an acceptable poem
They don't notch or groove in any way natural
Can't pronounce the profundity of quiet
or master the reverence with which I pierce it talking to you

I would never abandon us before you find me in you
I've lied to poor fools but you only get polished truth
Like how looking your way lights the most fiery quiet
By which we can see first and second sight entwine
Tying each other together as phenomena known natural
Harboring each other's home poem by poem

This poem is ours and to know that is natural
Unveiling how many sounds and spaces between are for you
'til the truth speaks loudly in our quiet entwine

ROAMING IN YOUR WILDS

The weatherman let me know
I'm under a heat dome
Frying by fair degrees more than normal
Evening brings no relief
The night sticking to you
I rambled unwilted all up and down the day
Bucked up against anyone who
reached for my reins

Now I'm sweating sundown
Buckets and sheets
Remembering a man who
ran right at my flank
Matching me jump for jump
Speed for speed
I reckon I'd haul it
wherever he leads

At least for a beautiful breakneck blaze
Thrashing across new thresholds while
burning skies overhang
At least, at last, let me, I ask
get a grip on where you're always running to
the frontiers and plains of escape
essential to discovering you

If you like my company and
I like roaming in your wilds
then we just gotta get good
at harnessing fires

Because the temperatures we generate
The chemicals we cook with
Leap in orange columns and white hot spires
Catching even from moonlight

Flinty earthen floor, magnetized to sparks
our parallel wild-eyed cantors give off
It's all going up tonight, going up between us
because we will it
Our sweltering shadow play perfectly backlit

HAVE TO BUT IT'S HARD

Walking circles around this little place
Feels like I'm doing laps in the pod

I know I have to but its hard to wait
for someone new to make me fall

It's cold outside and a furnace within
Feel so numb to everything but the steel of your skin

It's dangerous at night, going out or staying in
You used to make great company for giving into sin

Setting out into this backwards town
Feels like upside down is right side up

I know you have to but it's hard to take
when you revert back to acting tough

I'm older now and unafraid to take chances
Feel so numb to everything when you take full advantage

It's dangerous all the time, because *ohhh* you exist
Once that was my favorite fact, now running into you makes me flinch

CONCEPT OF LOVE

The inner critic won't shut up
He turns his withering bite
on the very concept of love
It's all so overheated
says this curmudgeon
who lives in me
You can't engage with love
and not turn corny
You might as well
rhyme *dream* with *sunbeam*
Might as well become partial
to long walks on the beach

Well, it so happens
I think it's important
to love and to be loved
Not to be sappy but
affection makes me happy
When someone pulls you to them
and you fit with them snugly
there's no more vivid sense
of actually belonging

So I won't resign to being post-love
I damn sure don't see myself
ever going post-sexual
My creator gave me the most
beautiful plethora of nerve endings
I believe they're meant to sing

Touch is just one of my methods of feeling
Feeling you out
Feeling you within
Exploring the intersections
of our distinct energies

Your tone of mind chiming, chiming
Your lifted lightform waving, inviting

You call to me
I don't know if you know it
You pronounce my favorite words
If I wasn't already a poet
I'd become one after
instinctive immersion
kicking in any time we kick back

No, love doesn't strike me
as corny today
It springs like an attack
I like it fine like that

SOLID HANG

What a glorious day
You remain a solid hang
I think I've come to count on
the nights with you too
even though it's not your responsibility
to help me stay sane

Saner, should say
Still been through the deranger
but my crazy is mostly innocuous
Some of these diagnoses
are superfluous

I'll keep it together easier now
Your recharge will coast me
for at least a couple days

I know you're person, not crystalline
I don't like you just for your energies
Tasty though they truly are

I'd feel better about an even exchange
so sup on my field, bro
Let's elevate art

ANYWHERE BUT SPLITSVILLE

If you won't get away from me
how can I concentrate
If you won't stay with me
let the feelings evaporate

I'm putting too much on you, I know
My needs are a mite contradictory
I run the good ones off
then cuss them for getting gone
That's the plot of my whole history

Why should it be
any different with you
Why should this ride
lead anywhere but Splitsville

I never told you I like flowers
They insult my manly powers
Fuck on outta here with your daffodils

For some reason you ain't scared
Our eyes lock stare to stare
Oh there are so many ways
loving each other could go *kerplooey*

If you dare I dare
to fan flames that flare
because in all my life, I swear
it's only you who ever knew me

INEXHAUSTIBLE

Hard in the paint, not even feeling faint
from spills I took, gravel I ate
In line to go again like I love the taste
They say if you won't
kill any part of you to survive
your hippy dippy self acceptance
will be the hill on which you die
Let's prove them wrong
Let's show them they lie

If we vibe you're my tribe
We traverse the same spaceways
If we're living we have a right to be alive
Gracing new arenas, earning new nicknames
If we slide the same way, don't swerve
We'll both hit the same nerve
By each other brothered, enamored, quenched, cured
Entangled on quantum levels
Our borders blurred

Down on your luck, I'll always give a fuck
Steep prices to pay, when is it enough
Leg breakers come collecting
Sent by balancers of cosmic scales
We'll blow them some raspberries or spin tall tales
They won't take your stroboscopic
core of light, Bossman, I'm telling you
There's no scenario where I'd let them
touch your essential cool

If a win gets under your skin
anytime you enlist assistance
Just know we both sweat the same bullets
Both dodge the same slugs, hunkered in
the same trenches
We exude complimentary polarities
Affect almost the exact same ambiance
Helping each other helps ourselves
Our symbiosis is obvious

What all this means, 'cos it's not for nothing,
is when we're holding hands
good fortune's not bluffing
You got this glow enhancing your
all-encompassing aura
I can't rebury anything it unearths in me
Some reservoir inexhaustible
Generates energy indefinitely

What it means is, stay, you're DNA
You're each next, vital breath
My fantastic, finest fate
Surprise, we're the same
so we might as well want to be
I wrote this to all of you
in hopes you'll take all of me

ABSTRACTION

I wish I had answers for you in this world
Right here in this dimensional abstraction
But even if I have no answers I'll still answer
when you need someone, anyone

ABOUT ATMOSPHERE PRESS

Founded in 2015, Atmosphere Press was built on the principles of Honesty, Transparency, Professionalism, Kindness, and Making Your Book Awesome. As an ethical and author-friendly hybrid press, we stay true to that founding mission today.

If you're a reader, enter our giveaway for a free book here:

SCAN TO ENTER
BOOK GIVEAWAY

If you're a writer, submit your manuscript for consideration here:

SCAN TO SUBMIT
MANUSCRIPT

And always feel free to visit Atmosphere Press and our authors online at atmospherepress.com. See you there soon!

ABOUT THE AUTHOR

For 26+ years, **TRAVIS HUPP** has been writing poetry about resilience, God, breaking free of oppressive structures, good trips, bad trips, love in its myriad forms, quantum physics, nature and the color blue, among other topics. *American Entropy* is his third book. His other two, *Faster, Annihilators!* And *Sin and I* are also available on Amazon.com and wherever books are sold.

www.ingramcontent.com/pod-product-compliance
Lightning Source LLC
LaVergne TN
LVHW041920070526
838199LV00051BA/2680